Adam's First Wife

Was She the Mother of the Human Race?

By Steve Preston

3rd Edition
2017

© Copyright 2009, Steve Preston
All rights reserved.
No part of this book may be reproduced, stored in a retrieval system, or transmitted by any means, electronic, mechanical, photocopying, recording, or otherwise, without written permission from the author.

2nd Edition 2012

Table of Contents

ADAM'S FIRST WIFE 1
    TABLE OF CONTENTS 3
    INTRODUCTION 5
    WHO WAS LILITH? 9
    THE BEGINNING 18
LILITH #1- NEPHILIMIC SCIENTIST WHO DEVELOPED MANY TYPES OF HUMANS 23
    GENETIC ENGINEER LILITH 24
    NEPHILIMIC BREEDING PROGRAM 32
    WERE THE TITANS AND NEPHILIM REAL?? 36
    INTELLIGENT NEPHILIM 50
    NOW FOR SOMETHING REALLY STRANGE 60
    LILITH MADE HOMO-HABILIS 66
    NEPHILIM/LILITH WANTED A SERVANT 74
    WORLD VIEW OF HOMO-ERECTUS 79
    GOD RESTED AND LILITH WORKED 88
    LILITH'S BEST CREATION NEANDERTHAL 96
    NEANDERTHAL GOT TOO SMART 113
LILITH #2- NEPHILIMIC WIFE TO ADAM, CONSORT TO SAMAEL, REPTILIAN SHAPESHIFTER, AND "FATHER" TO CAIN 114
    LILITH, ADAM'S 1ST WIFE 115
    DESCRIPTIONS OF LILITH 124
    PICTURES OF LILITH 130
    DIFFICULTY WITH SEX 135
    LILITH CAME BACK 137
    LILITH IN THE GARDEN 139
    LILITH HANDS OUT FRUIT 143
    EVE SEDUCED BY A SERPENT 145
    SERPENT HALF-BREED 149
    ADAM AND EVE FIND A FIG LEAF 152
    THE SERPENT WASN'T A SNAKE 154
    LILITH THE SERAPHIMIC NEPHILIM 156
    ADAM AND LILITH 163
DESCENDANTS OF LILITH 166
    LIVING WITH THE CURSE 167
    FAMILIES OF LILITH DESCENDANTS 175
    SERPENT GODS 184
LILITH#3 AS A DEMONESS 189

LILITH#3 IN THE CABBALA	190
LILITH THE EVIL SPIRIT	194
LILITH REMEDY	199
DEMONIC LILITH CHARACTERS	201
CONCLUSION	204
ABOUT THE AUTHOR	207

Introduction

This book is not about Eve. Instead, it is about the woman that was made when Adam was made or before he was made. Her name was Lilith. If you have ever wondered about Genesis story with respect to Adam trying to find a helpmate; this will help you understand. God did not forget to make a woman for Adam, nor did Adam, initially, go around a see if any of the animals were compatible with him as a mate.

> ***Genesis 2:18-20*** *And the LORD God said, It is not good that the man should be alone; <u>I will make him an helpmeet</u>. And out of the ground the LORD God formed every beast of the field, and every fowl of the air; and brought them unto Adam - but for Adam there was not found an <u>helpmeet</u> for him.*

By the way, Adam quickly determined that the skunk would not make a good helpmeet. It took him a week before the other animals would let him come near them.

Also, I must tell you, snakes did not have legs or talk in the Garden of Eden. The Bible doesn't say that, so don't go believing that the Bible is wrong in its description of Adam and the whole Garden of Eden visual description as laid out by Moses.

To make this all make sense, I will have to first describe a group of humans that came before Adam; discuss capabilities of these people that were pretty spectacular; and only then can I bring you up to speed with Adam's first wife. While she is named Lilith in many of the ancient Jewish texts she had other names in other histories. It is quite easy to tell that all are describing the same person. To make the description of his first wife more confusing, There seems to be 3 different depictions of his wife. The one we will concentrate on is the one who could be called the mother of the Gentiles. Let me just give you a quick rundown from Jewish texts. While I mostly show the Moses description, there are dozens more and we will review them for a comparative analysis to understand who Lilith was.

Section 1 Lilith#1

- **Genesis 6 and Jeremiah 4-** During the Mesozoic Era, Giant humans created a high level of civilization and slowly began dying to become angels living in heaven. *Jeremiah 4:23-27-[near the end of the wars] "I beheld the Earth, and, lo, it was without form, and void; and the heavens, and they had no light. I beheld, and, lo, there was no man, and all the cities thereof were broken down."*[Cities of the people of the Mesozoic Era]
- **Genesis 1:1 and Isaiah 9-**The Angels began missing "CARNAL" living and revolted. A third of the inhabitants of Heaven became human again as punishment. They were called Nephilim people and Lilith was one of them. *Isaiah 9:17-21---`Is this the man [leader of the rebel angels] – who made the world like a desert and overthrew its cities, All the kings of the nations [Mesozoic Giant Kings] lie in glory,*

- *Genesis 1:24-* Nephilim scientists called "Lilith" modified Apes to develop Ape-men like Homo-Habilis ape-men.
- *Genesis 1:27:* God Created a new human and Nephilimic scientists called "Lilith" modified this human to make him a better servant to establish Neanderthal humans.

Section 2 Lilith#2

- *Genesis 2:7-* Adam was created and Lilith became his wife. Jewish text tell us "*she was made from impure sediment*"- possibly a reference to her being a Nephilim female.
- *Genesis 2:18-*Lilith got angry with Adam for not allowing her to have a superior position to him she left for a time.
- *Genesis 2:20-* Adam got lonely so Eve was cloned from him.
- *Genesis 3:13* Lilith came back and, somehow, joined with a Nephilim named Samael to become the reptilian-conjurer who seduced and impregnated Eve.
- *Genesis 3:7* Then the "conjurer/serpent" [same Hebrew word] convinced Eve to eat a forbidden fruit and Adam did the same. The conjurer was punished with three main items and Adam's wife had a couple punishments
- *Genesis 3:14-* The Conjurer would have to eat the dust of the Earth.
- *Genesis 3:15-* The Conjurer's "seed" would <u>no longer</u> be able to join with Eve's seed. [This indicated she had gotten pregnant, from the Nephilim, but never again.]
- *Genesis 3:15-* The Conjurer would be abhorred by other humans
- *Genesis3:16-* Eve's desire would turn from the Conjurer

- *Genesis 3:16-* Eve would be sad after conception [nothing about pain]
- *Genesis 4:1-2-* Eve was pregnant from the seduction and had Cain and Lebudah, then she had Abel and another girl, presumably, from Adam.
- *Genesis 4:16-* Cain left with his twin sister, Lebudah, after killing Abel who was supposed to marry her.
- *Genesis 4:22-* Because of the punishment, Nephilim could not mate with Adamics, but the lineage of Cain was different. Lilith tried to have children by Cain. Initially that did not work, but after a long time, Lilith, called Zillah, had Naamah and Tubal-Cain.
- *Zohar 1:5-55-* All the children of Naamah and Tubal-Cain became demons just like the other Nephilim, but the other descendants of the half breed Cain became Gentile humans.

Section 3 Lilith as a Demoness

- *Genesis 4:20-* After Lilith died she became a demon and continuously forced Adam to be with her and her daughter Naamah
- *Genesis 4:25-* after 130 "Jubilee"-years, Adam had a son by Eve named Seth and 60 other children.
- *Bacharach 19-* After the Pleistocene Extinction, Lilith died and became the Master of demons. *"The demoness Lilith seduces sleeping men and then kills them if she can."* Sumerians called the demons Lila and Jewish people called them Lilin.

With that level of confusion let's get started.

Who Was Lilith?

If you have never heard of Lilith, I know that you are wondering just what this "Mother of the Human Race" is all about. Everyone, or almost everyone, believes that Eve, "wife of Adam" should have that distinction. That is generally, what the Biblical writings say but Eve was not the only one to have children by Adam and she was not the only woman married to him. In fact, some texts have the number of children Adam had was 60, or more. The one called Cain was most likely the son of Lilith. Later we find that Lilith tries to procreate with Cain and for a long time she is unsuccessful. Finally, she has children by him. Cain's non-mother wife, Lebudah, also has children by this man and together, these 2 women can be considered the mothers of the Gentile races.

This is not a story that goes against the Biblical foundations, but rather, it expands the details. After saying that, I must also say that there must be some validity in the ancient stories about a godlike female named Lilith. I think the details will surprise and enlighten you. Before we start, let me tell you about the 3 distinct entities associated with Lilith that I alluded to earlier. We will be looking the history and the story associated with each one of those listed below.

Lilith #1 [Genetic Engineer]

This is the Nephilimic human mother of mankind identified around the world. Without getting into a lot of detail, a Nephilim was a human that lived on earth long before the Cro-Magnon People associated with the one we call Adam. Before Adam, the Nephilim female scientists would have children with or modify the Early humans identified in Genesis 1:27. After a number of modifications, the most advanced of these people were known as the Neanderthal. The thing to know about Neanderthal is their brains were 15% larger than our modern brains so they were not humped over and grunting like an ape. We are told they red reddish hair and has a light complexion. With that massive brain, we can believe they also were smart and had their own language. The genetic Engineering Lilith is not the one we will concentrate on, but I will provide some of the ancient texts concerning her.

Extremely long lives

Many of the ancient texts describe lifetimes that seem unbelievable to us today. We are told one of the reasons that ancient humans lived so very, very long was a special food sometimes referred to as the fruit of the tree of life. The book Enoch indicated the fruit tree looked like a Tamarind and the fruit was grape-like, but don't go fill up with grapes just yet. I know that you have probably been wondering why this tree was in the Garden of Eden in the first place and Adam evidently ate from it until he was kicked out and the Nephilim people who remained used it to supply life giving fruit. I will not be going over the fruit thing in this book except for some cursory statements. Even though I will not be examining how they lived so long, bear in mind that these individuals would live for many thousands of years and so did Adam. Two books used by the early Christians, "Adam and Eve I and II", both indicated Adam lived 5500 years after the birth of Seth. The book of Esdras gave us details which point to a creation of Adam about 35 thousand years ago, and using the common Jewish Jubilee-year as reference, Genesis indicated Adam lived about 930 Jubilee-years, or 6500 years, and would have been created about 35 thousand years ago, exactly as the other histories described and it confirms to the mysterious creation of the Cro-Magnon humans that so confuse scientists.

Lilith#2 [Shapeshifting Reptilian-human wife of Adam]

This is the Lilith you see in so many paintings of Adam and Eve being given the "wisdom-fruit" by a half human female – serpent. She was able to turn into a reptile according to many ancient texts including Sumerian, Egyptian, Jewish, and other histories. According to various histories, this Lilith also had sexual relations with the other humans of the day and the offspring were---let's say different. This version of Lilith will be investigated to establish why this strange concept arose and what portions might have portions of truth.

Lilith #3 [Evil Demoness]

After Lilith #2 died, she came back with the same punishment that Satan and his followers had. She became a demoness. In fact, she came back as the queen of the demons who would take little children and seduce men only to kill them later. This Lilith character was also known around the world with names like succubus, but the character was always the same. While this is an interesting concept, this work does not go into the details of this emanation beyond providing some of the ancient texts describing Lilith to give you some level of insight.

Timeline of the Book

If that hasn't scared you away from reading and learning about this mother of humanity, let me go over the timeline of this book to possibly confuse you some more.

__180,000 Years ago-Cretaceous Age__-Humans have been on the earth for thousands of years. How they got here will not be covered, but it is my belief that the Creator God simply put them on the earth. There is a tremendous amount of proof considering how long ago this was, so we can believe there were millions of people living during this time. We will get to some of the proof of their advance civilization and character.

Timing Correction-Today, scientists know that nuclear decay timing horribly flawed, but it is still described in our schools. To gain a much better comparatively confirmed dating, CO_2 cyclic Ice Core dating, O_{16} density cyclic dating, Hawaiian hotspot travel dating, and archeo-magnetic direction cyclic dating from the mid-Atlantic volcanic action. Confirmation of all 4 methods tell us the Jurassic ending happened 240 thousand years ago, Cretaceous Extinction happened 120 thousand years ago, and the Pleistocene Extinction and worldwide flood occurred 10 thousand years ago.

__120,000 Years ago-Cretaceous Extinction__- A huge war left the Earth destroyed and the losers were banished to Earth forever and became the Nephilim people. Being forced to stay here, after they died, they came back as something called demons. This was known to science as the Cretaceous Extinction

__100,000 Years ago-Early-Tertiary Period__-Back on Earth, the Nephilim people gained a huge amount of knowledge

concerning living longer and genetic manipulation. This only makes sense as we have gained a considerable amount of knowledge in those areas in the very short "modern times" and researchers are finding hundreds of unfossilized T-rex and similar dinosaurs that were regenerated about 20 thousand years ago so the cells and membranes are still flexible. A tiny grouping of the extraordinary unfossilized dinosaur remains are shown below.

Soon, most of the animals of the Pleistocene were called abominations or Unclean animals and scientists like Lilith were responsible for their manufacture.

80,000 Years ago-Mid-Tertiary Period-*One of the genetic experiments was the changing of apes into ape-men. After many changes, these ancient humans began using their own DNA as a change catalyst. They may have even had sex with the experiments. The result was somewhat better ape-like animals.* In this book, I personify the genetic breeders as Liliths and she may very well have been one of these scientists.

Ancient texts tell us, even this new man was not helpful in doing work for the ancient humans so God created a new human, possibly with the help of the ancient scientists like our Lilith character. This was the Homo-Erectus, the first true human not associated with the ancient humans. The Bible calls this time the 6th Age. Genetic scientists like Lilith continued experimenting to make the Neanderthal as I previously showed.

60,000 Years ago-Later Tertiary Period- *The ancient humans that would become demons [Jews called them Nephilim] bred with these humans and produced many different strains. [We called the breeder Lilith]. One of these hybrid humans was called the Neanderthal man. He was a great worker, but not creative in any way. He also lacked appreciation of the Nephilim scientist for "modifying him".*

40,000 Years ago-Beginning of the Pleistocene Age-*God was not impressed with the work that the Nephilim [like Lilith] were doing and he created still another human [ADAM] with special qualities including an internal spirit could leave the Earth after dying.] [I know you believe that Adam was here only 6 to 8 thousand years ago, but evidence not covered in this book indicates the much older date—by the way, the date is not important for the Lilith story. Scientists called this man Cro-Magnon.]-The Nephilim were at it again and one named Lilith bred with this new ADAMIC man. God put a stop to the Lilith cohabitation with the purebred Adamics after the Garden of Eden fruit incident, but the hybrid humans could mate with the Adamics and they did-many times.*

10,000 Years ago-Pleistocene Extinction-Gentiles-*Most of the people of that time were from the union of Lilith or others like her that cohabitated with the Adamics. These people were called Gentiles. A small group of Adamic humans stayed away from the outsiders were considered the Chosen*

Ones. –I bet you always wondered why only a few people are considered the chosen ones and the rest of us were designated as "Gentile". If you wondered about it, the answer is not that pleasant. If you are a gentile, you are not a pure blooded Adamic human.

The Earth axis shifted forcing huge tidal waves, rain, Earthquakes and destruction around the world and the pole melted and refroze. Noah and his family were the only chosen ones [pure Adamics] to survive the flood. That is not to say, his family was the only surviving group of hybrid humans. Australian kangaroo were deposited by Australian Gentile or Nephilim human survivors. They did not hop all the way from Noah to Australia without leaving offspring along the way.

8,000 Years ago-Early Holocene Age- Ubaid People-*After the flood, The descendants of Lilith who survived looked different than other humans. These group of humans would have been the cursed descendants of the "Reptilian-Lilith" who had given Adam the Tree-of-knowledge-fruit". For this crime they were changed to always appear reptilian.* I will show the evidence that this group lived among the "normal humans". They lived, worked, had babies, and were, evidently, at peace with the "normal" humans for many years. Typically, these Lilith descendants are called Ubaid people, their reptilian features were unmistakable, but many do not know where they came from or what happened to them.

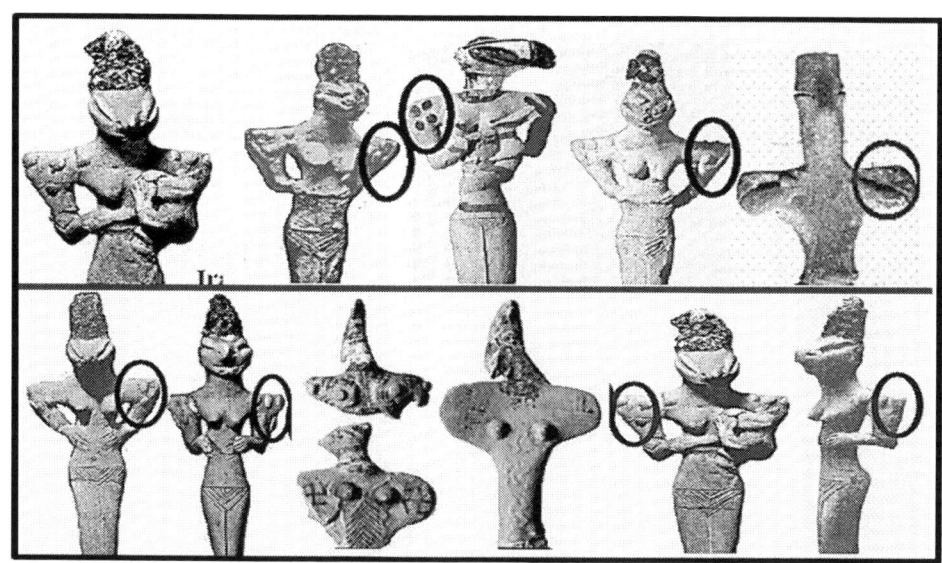

These lizard people images can be found around the world so we can be pretty sure at least some of them survived the Pleistocene extinction.

6,000 years ago-Lilith Demons-*By this time Lilith and her offspring had died. Her offspring were bound to the earth because of the punishments of God. According to many texts, these spirits continued to tempt men and do other generally evil things. I will show that this was a widespread belief of the Jewish community and that it spread to many others around the world.*

The Beginning

Most of you have seen the many depictions of the serpent in the Garden of Eden that was responsible for "tempting" Eve which eventually led to troubles. The one below is similar to most in that the half human half snakelike being doing the tempting is female. This female and the almost unbelievable evidence about her existence is what this book is about. That female being was named Lilith by the ancient Jewish community and she was not always a reptile, but she could appear as reptilian according to a number of accounts. Not so much like the image below used in 16th Century paintings. More like human with reptilian features.

As I said previously, the first incantation of Lilith will be addressed before we get to the snake-woman because the evidence of her existence and the effects of her existence come first in our history.

While many have never heard about the ancient Jewish hero/demon named Lilith, she was an important part of the ancient Jewish religion and life. Stories about all three Lilith's were not only widely accepted in the Jewish community, but also, the traits of Lilith were transferred over to other historical writings either by association or recognition of a real entity.

This book examines what has been said about Lilith and similarities with other heroine of the ancient world. It also proposes a logical progression of details and theories that make the various histories, science and theology work together.

Are Ancient Histories Wrong?

If one assumes that all historical data presented in classroom texts is correct, you are thinking I'm a crazy man, but the more concurrence we have of similar accounts around the world the more likely the data is not fabricated or imagined to enhance a particular ruler or society. The essence of the Lilith story must contain a reasonable amount of truth and, hopefully, I have established, in this work, a beginning from which the reader can glean the essence of our true history with respect to the one known as Lilith.

According to ancient texts, she was powerful, cunning, and sometimes evil. By many accounts, she was involved in the creation of mankind. This may not sit well with some people, so if you already believe that the information will be twisted to create some esoteric dilemma in the "known" areas of our past, PLEASE put this book down right now and go about your life without this level of insight. If you believe that some of the ancient texts could, very well, have been written in an attempt to tell "truth" rather than scandal, please continue and learn about the one called Lilith.

She may have lived over 50 thousand years ago. If you have not read my other works on the history of mankind, this detail may make you believe that she was one of those Neanderthal humans you keep hearing about, but she was not. In fact, she may not have been completely human, at least not human in the way we limit human capability today. I know! The tail gave it away, but I'm not talking about an artist's rendition of what he wanted to portray. I'm talking about logic and historical evidence. As I briefly mentioned in the introduction, Lilith was, apparently, one of a special group of humans called Nephilim, by the ancient Jews or called Annunaki, by the ancient Sumerians. For those who survived the flood, the Jews renamed this group the ANAK and the Anakim. The Egyptians called them Lords of the Amenti and the people of India called them Arya [Copper men]. In the Americas, the Mongulala called them Akamim while the Adena of the Ohio Valley called them the Archaics.

Nephilim Gods

So revered were these ancient people that they were worshipped as gods. The antics and capabilities of these people were the backdrop components used by the Greeks when establishing their history of the Greek gods. I know you were told that the whole gods and goddesses thing was a fairy tale but let me tell you this. It was way too difficult to write things down in the old days to waste them on fairy tales. The other thing to notice is that the gods and goddesses were all human-like for a reason. The obvious reason was that they were humans. The Nephilim humans ruled over the other humans for many, many years. After a lot of time had gone by, they finally died off and people wrote down the ancient stories of their lives, capabilities, and frailties to preserve their history. Surely, the stories of these ancient people have been embellished over the years, but there is no reason to believe that ancient people would create gods in their own minds that would have so many shortcomings unless there were shortcomings to find. After all these people believed that the "gods" could kill them at any moment. Would you characterize a powerful being as ugly, or lecherous, or stupid, or any of the other strange qualities of the thousands of ancient god characters unless a couple of things had been true. The two things I'm referring to are that the "god" actually had that characteristic and "most importantly" that the "so called god" had already died. The second one was the most important one.

It is apparent that these Nephilim were very similar to humans of today in many ways. One of those ways is that they eventually died.

They lived, breathed, ate, married, had children, became jealous, had affairs, were afraid, became angry, and killed, helped, healed, taught, ruled, and died. Even though they died, they lived for enormous lengths of time and they were revered as gods.

I know all this multiple types of humans is confusing, but the big difference between Titan/Homo-Gigantus people who lived with the dinosaurs, and Nephilim/Homo-Capensis people who regenerated dinosaurs during the Pleistocene was that Titans were during the Cretaceous and the name was changed after the Cretaceous Extinction. Generally speaking, the Nephilim people were called Anak humans after the Pleistocene Extinction, but all can be traced to a common group. In this book I will treat them as the same even with the slight differences, However, we will describe one severe difference between Titans and Nephilim and that is when Nephilim died, they became demons. When we look at Lilith dying, we are told she became one of the leading demonesses.

The graphic below tries to characterize the various Lilith descriptions and physical evidence.

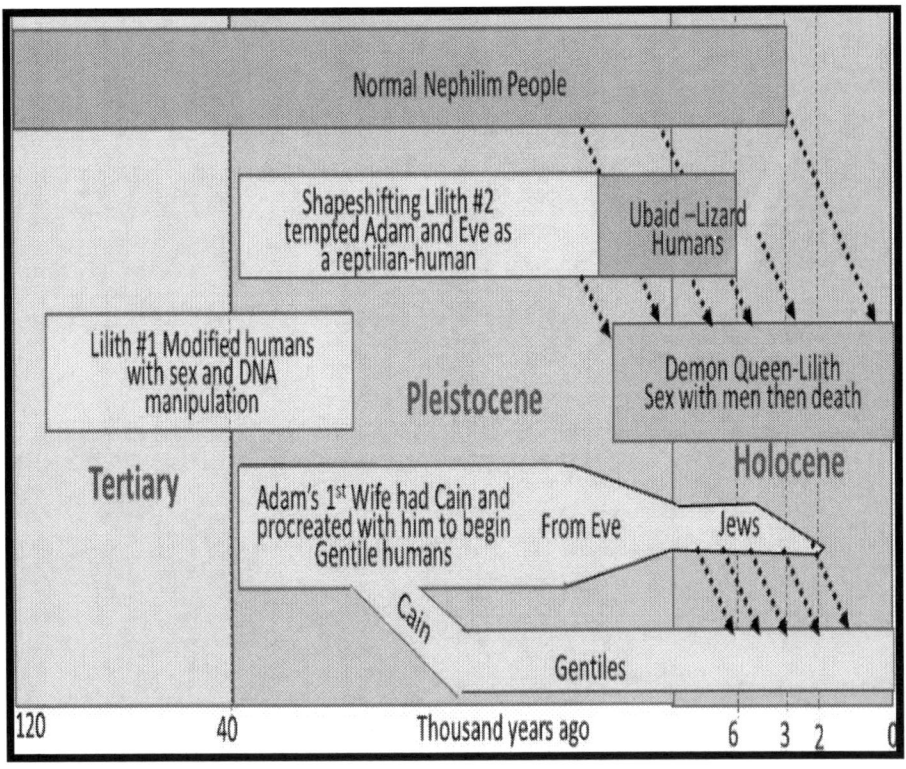

Lilith #1 - Nephilimic Scientist who developed many types of Humans

Genetic Engineer Lilith

I'm sorry about the off track discussion about gods, but before we can go very far in our quest to understand why so many wrote about this Lilith character, we must first understand the concept or reality of an ancient "pre-man" the ancient Jewish writers called Nephilim. He wasn't a real god, but evidence suggests that he was powerful. Evidence further confirms that this human was real and worshipped as a god while he lived with the "normal humans". Along with the previous chart, the chart below may help you understand the various human and humanoid beings described in our Bible. In this chart Nephilim are called Anak and by the Scientific name Homo Capensis.

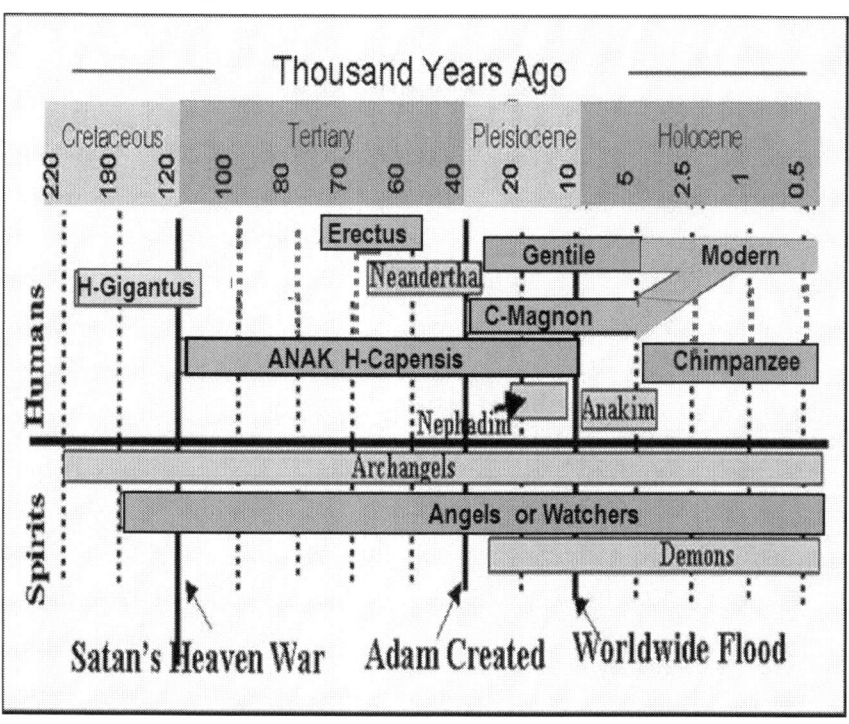

Adam and his direct line of descendants are called by the scientific name Cro-Magnon in the Chart as well. These Nephilim are not easy to ignore in our ancient history and have been called many names. Hundreds of texts talk about them and even ancient artifacts that attest to the fact that there were beings on earth for a hundred thousand years before the Nephilim called Homo Gigantus or Titan. Apparently, the H. Gigantus, followed by the H. Capensis were the rulers of the ancient world. By the way; Gigantus simply means Giant, Capensis means long-headed giant, Nephilim meant "Thrown out of Heaven, Anunnaki meant "Came from Heaven", Anak meant "Long Necked or headed Giant". Arya meant "Metal "reddish" Men", and Archaic meant "Ancient One". A good example of distant descendants of these people has been found in Peru where 300, ancient, red-haired, long-headed skulls. Later, similar Capensis type skulls were found in Egypt, Russia, U.S.A., Malta, and other parts of the world. These were humans related to the Nephilim/Anak of whom Lilith was a member by all accounts. Let me apologize right now for this section having to be rather lengthy. Without this background, the life of Lilith will not be well understood.

Nephilim Ate Right

By all accounts, their life-spans were **very** long and were aided by a strange fruit from something the ancient Jews called the tree-of-life. Dozens of civilizations around the world told almost identical stories including the need to use some special food to stay young. In addition to special food, there may have been another aid in keeping these humans younger. We will discuss this other method briefly later in the book. The people of Mesoamerica told similar stories without the pleasure of being able to compare histories with the Greeks and Jews.

Like the Lilith Stories, the ancient stories of the Nephilim are astoundingly similar, while this is not the story to be told here, this beginning is necessary to establish the backdrop for a real discussion about Lilith. The Lilith story begins during the time when the Nephilim were in power. In order to exact some reasonable detail, we will confine this history to that evolving around Lilith only.

If we are to believe the many stories of this Nephilim, one depiction of Lilith was that of a genetic engineer of sorts and "her" story begins, perhaps, over 100 thousand years ago. [I told you these guys lived a long time.]. According to texts around the world, she or someone similar to her was credited for manufacturing a hybrid human—part modern man; part Nephilim. [By the way, there could have been a number of similar beings that were all identified as Lilith so we aren't simply talking about a person, but an icon of sorts.]

Nephilim Took God's Place

After aiding in the "evolution of man" Nephilim, evidently led the "normal humans" away from the creator God so that the Nephilim could take God's place.

Essene [Baptizing Jews and first Christians] Text

Lamentation of Jared*-And the gods came to the Earth and lead astray HIS [God's] own tribe of Adam and those of Cain.* [This seems to indicate that Cain's tribe was not from Adam but from Lilith. It is a representation of the Nephilim leading the humans astray.]

Egyptian Text

Emerald Tablets*-Seven Lords of Amenti, children of the morning, masters of wisdom, formless, teachers of the children of men, from them came the keys to hidden magic, from them came the instruments of power.* [These Lords of Amenti may have been the Nephilim that taught humans inappropriate things.]

Nephilim Taught Man

Man, with the instruction of the Nephilim, made all types of things. The Inca indicated that with the help of "the outsiders [Nephilim] they were able to learn science, sorcery, and finally, flying. This same account occurred around the world. Many accounts of flying machines have been recorded in the histories from India, Chaldea, Babylon, Egypt, China, Sumeria, and other places around the world. These are not covered in this book, but the evidence is astounding. Evidently, God condoned none of this information transfer, but the Nephilim continued to teach and the different types of humans all seemed to listen intently. The chart below shows the non-Cro Magnon humans we have found so far and where we found the bones. The Bible indicated God put enmity between the seed of the Conjurer/serpent and the Cro-Magnon so there were no offspring. A number of Jewish text indicated the Conjurer was the dual Nephilim union of Lilith and Samael] That being said, we find in a number of texts that Lilith at first could not copulate with Cain initially, but after a while, she could produce little Gentile boys and girls. As the land of Nod might have been a simple description of sexual friendliness of Cain and his descendants with the other people of that time [Neanderthal etc.], we can believe some of the Gentiles were mixed with some of the other humans shown in the chart but main location of discovery.

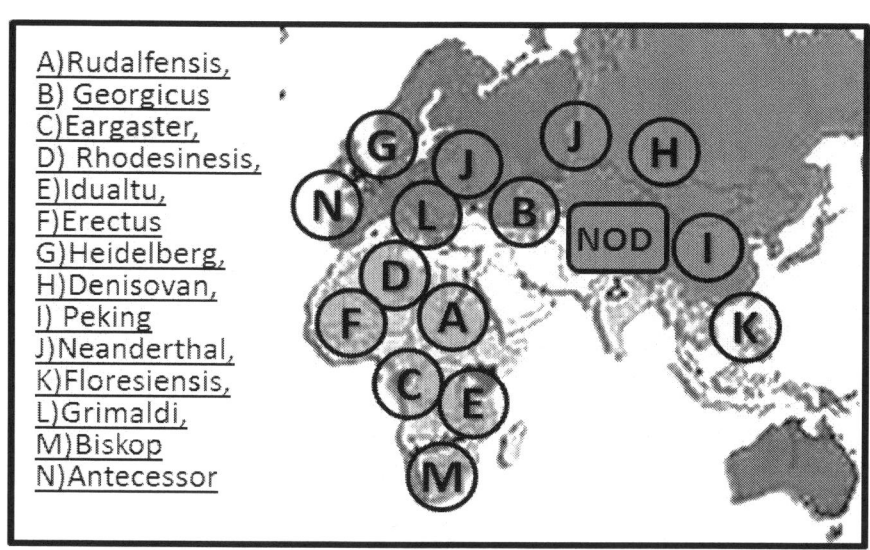

Great Men of Old

The incident with the Tree of Knowledge was a wakeup call for the Cro-Magnon, but still, men continued to listen to and learn from the Nephilim. I sense there is confusion, so let me readdress the condition of the world at this time.

Genesis 1:28, Isaiah 9:17-21 Jubilees 2:9, Jeremiah 4:23-27- *The Titan giants had all died in the Cretaceous and disappeared during the Cretaceous extinction. Those who survived were now called Homo-Capensis or Nephilim.*

Genesis 1:26*-Nephilim began modifying Ape DNA. The best they could come with was Homo-Habilis.*

Genesis 1:27*-Nephilim wanted a better servant so God created Homo Erectus, but they modified H. Erectus to make Neanderthal.*

Genesis 2:7- *Much later God created a new man [Cro-Magnon]*

Genesis 3:15*-Lilith/Samael had Cain by Eve before a curse was placed on the Nephilim that would not allow Man's seed to mix with Nephilim.*

Zohar 1:19*-Cain was different and Lilith was able to breed with his people to make the group called Gentiles. When Lilith died she became a Demoness.*

Nephilim Were the Greek Gods

The Greeks may have been more correct than we would like to believe in their depictions of these ancient humans.

Following is a collage of Greek gods and goddesses. The thing to note is that these creatures were just like us and in many ways, worse. Many Nephilim were vainer, more lustful, and pettier than normal humans as shown in the various artworks below.

Nephilim Sex

Of course, the Greek gods had sex with humans; a lot of sex, but that concept is not foreign to the other ancient stories, so we should not simply discount the notion because it makes us uncomfortable. Here are a few examples.

The Gandharvas *[sort of like gods] in Hindu traditions were considered musicians of the heavens and controlled rain. They had only one real flaw, however, they loved sex. The ancient Hindu priests had special incantations to ward off these intruding beings during times of sacred procedures.*

In Zoroastrian texts, *the Archeon are angelic-like beings with a problem—sex.*

In Jewish texts *["Book of Enoch"], the angel Azazel and his 200 followers had one major problem-sex.*

In the Koran *we find two angelic beings; Harut and Marut. They both had one problem-sex.*

With all this sex, there were probably babies. We will get to that later and yes there were. We will later find Cain was the child of Eve and Lilith and many offspring of unions between Nephilim, like Lilith and Cain's offspring assured substantial trouble. God had enough and finally destroyed the Earth, but let's see how One named Lilith began breeding many different humanoids and humans.

Note: This first Lilith is not a specific person. Shae was a scientists or many, many scientists who modified animals and humans.

Nephilimic Breeding Program

As we look into a brief history of the Lilith #1 genetic breeder, we need to look at artifacts and scientific presumptions. Scientists help us establish the idea that some external character "bred" humans as a critical part of human evolution. When I talk about breeding, I'm talking about Lilith again, so continue to see a female in the back of your mind as we go through this book. The highest achievement of Nephilim was Neanderthal. While we were told in school the thing grunted, clubbed women over the head, came out of Africa, had a dark complexion, and lived in caves, DNA studies now show Neanderthal had a larger brain than modern humans, was not associated with African Erectus directly, had a light complexion, red hair, a tenor voice, and a language. He was not the image to the left taught in school.

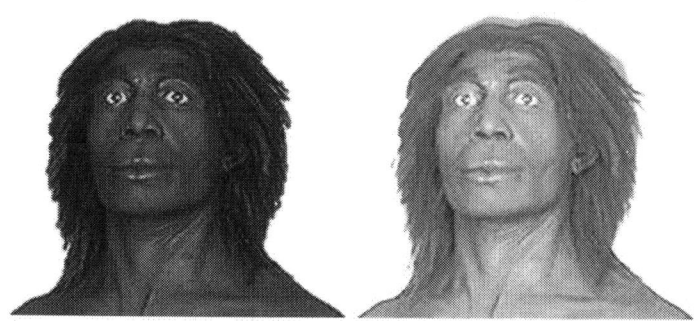

The evolution of man has been studies for hundreds of years, but the evidence of several huge jumps in this evolution process are typically not addressed adequately. Today some scientists try to characterize the evolution process as something that could provide major changes instantaneously, but survival of grossly different beings after this type of change would depend on many, many identical "jumps" occurring at the same time and in the same vicinity. I know it's hard to believe, but how else could evolutionary changed have occurred? The jump I will concentrate on right now is the huge jump from what is called Homo-Habilis [Nephilimic modified ape] to Homo-Erectus [the first non-Nephilimic man]. A second huge jump from Homo-erectus to Neanderthalis will also have to be investigated as well along with a jump from Homo-Erectus to the modern man. The real Neanderthal image is provided above right. He was substantially different than modern humans, but substantially different from the Homo-Erectus also. He was not, however a freak of nature, he was a calculated experiment to establish a specific set of traits and Lilith was the curator. Later the Habilis and Erectus images will be shown for comparison and contention.

Without outside influences such as a genetic scientist providing for the identical stimulus to many embryos, I just can't understand how the remarkable changes occurred. These humans went from this almost completely ape creature called Pro-Consul to modern man in less than 70 thousand years. I know the time seems too short, so let's consider the outside manipulation.

There is strange and compelling evidence that "fully civilized" humans lived on earth during the Cretaceous. Dozens and dozens of artifacts attest to this almost certain occurrence. We will look at some of these findings, but there are many others we will not address here. This is a very important concept that must be understood if an understanding of evolution and the acts of Lilith can be addressed.

The evidence of these humans seems to get less abundant as we get closer to the time of Neanderthal. They seemed to go away and leave less civilized humans in their place. The reasons for this decrease in the population of these ancient people is not the topic of this book, but it should be noted that the number of individuals decreased but there was still a relatively large population of the ancient humans that survived and helped in the expansion of the modern human when he came into the picture some 40 thousand years ago.

The brain size of Homo-Habilis is only ½ the size of the Homo-Erectus and that is only ½ the size of Neanderthalis.

As we move to the modern man, the brain size actually shrinks a little. These jumps are very curious in that other areas of the body had little or no modification. It was like the brain evolved separately from the rest of the human. Of course, the brain was not evolving; its make-up was being manipulated by genetic experiments.

If we look at Proconsul, [Ancestral Ape] the brain size remains about the same until today when compared with modern apes. This is also curious in that it appears that most of the other animals had very little change in enhancement of thought process. This is what one would expect from evolution-minor changes that could be supported by the normal populations.

> *In fact, you might not realize this, but the very ancient Amoeba is still alive today and in the same state that they were millions of years ago. Now that is what I call evolution.*

The weirdness that is forced on us by the uncontrolled evolutionists can be reduced if we insert an entity we will call Lilith. While I am not talking about a specific person, I am talking about these Nephilimic humans manipulating the humanoid creatures of the day to artificially "develop" it or him. ---Wait a minute; I'm getting ahead of myself. Let's first start with the Nephilimic humans.

Were the Titans and Nephilim Real??

The first two questions about Titans [Homo-Gigantus] and Nephilim [Homo-Capensis] Humans are, "Were they real?", and, "Where did they come from?" The beginnings of these ancient humans are not the topic of this book. My personal belief is that they were created by our God, but you can bring on little green men or whatever you like. Let's just say that they got here [over 150 thousand years ago] some way and influenced the development of other creatures. The whole concept of these ancient humans and any "evidence" to suggest that they were here seem like lies or misinterpretations of artifacts, but there are simply too many incidences to ignore. Below are a few of the hundreds of pieces of evidence, but remember this is simply a sampling of the many pieces that suggest that Nephilim humans were here a long time ago and they were human.

Standard Geological Timeline		
Era/Period/Epoch	Time (M yrs. ago)	Time (T yrs. ago)
Archaeozoic Period	5000-1500	50,000-3000
Proterozoic Period	1500-545	3000-1000
Cambrian period	550-500	1000-900
Ordovician period	500-440	900-800
Silurian period	440-410	800-700
Devonian period	410-365	700-600
Carboniferous	365-300	600-500
Permian period	300-250	500-400
Triassic period	250-212	400-300
Jurassic period	212-145	300-200
Cretaceous period	145-65	200-100
Tertiary period	65-1.8	100-40
Pleistocene period	1.8-0.01	40-10
Holocene period	0.01-0	10-00

Before we get to this evidence, let me re train you concerning timing just a little.

The preceding chart has the previously established dating in the middle and the newly reconstructed dated established after nuclear decay dating was proven to have a **_5000% variance_** and usually showed dates that were much older than known date.

The newer dating uses 4 different cross compared dating methods including Ice Core samples of dust and CO_2 cycles, Hawaiian Island hotspot movement tracking, Archaeomagnetic field cycling from the mid-Atlantic Crest and the cyclic O_{18} levels found in Greenland. Please disregard Nuclear decay timing assertions, especially those beyond about 30 thousand years.

Nephilim in America

Nevada 1927-A sandal sole print was found in a coal seam. Even the impressions of the threading holding the shoe together could be discerned. Estimated age of the shoeprint was Cretaceous. It had to be <u>before the coal was coal</u>. [See the cretaceous fossil left below]

Washington State-The photo [preceding right] was taken in northern Washington State and was reportedly found with another partial imprint. It is the 16-inch long shoe print of a large individual. The rock itself was determined to be <u>Tertiary</u>.

Utah-1968-The picture below is of a fossilized, 10-½ inch long Nephilimic human sandal print found next to a small human's footprints. Two live trilobites were crushed by the sandal in the same stone before fossilization. Columbia Union College made studies on the fossil an attested to its authenticity. The age is Cretaceous or older. The circles show the locations of the unfortunate trilobite carcasses.

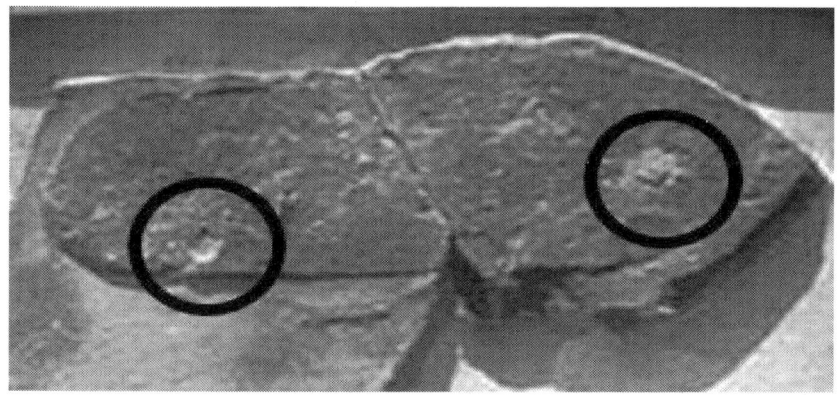

Bare Feet

Most of the hundreds of unbelievably ancient prints being found are of barefooted humans, but the prints leave no mistake. Most of these creatures were "human" just like you or me. Even children's footprints have been found attesting to the fact that normal procreation was evident during this time and the beings were not angels or what we classify as angels today. Here are a few examples.

New Mexico-The following Nephilimic human footprint found in what is believed to be the Permian layer before the Dinosaurs. Estimated age is Cretaceous.

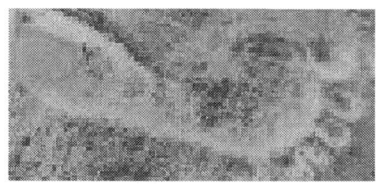

Utah 1969-More footprints found near Salt Lake City- 2 more sandal prints were found with trilobite fossils nearby. The estimated age is Cretaceous. [There must have been a large settlement in the area for so many footprints to be found.]

Arizona 1968-A small child's 6-½ inch long footprint was found in bed of Shale. Estimated age of the shale was Cretaceous.

Missouri 1822-This is a drawing [below left] of a footprint found in a slab of limestone. The prints were 10 ½ inches long and were estimated to be Cretaceous.

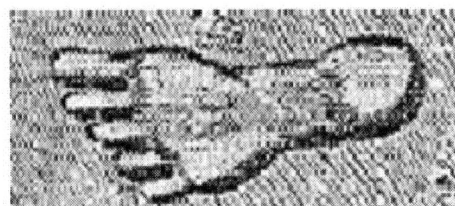 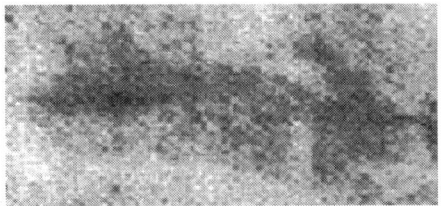

Missouri 1970-Footprints were found in a rock quarry. Estimated age was Tertiary. [See above right]

Oklahoma and Wisconsin-Evidence of Tertiary footprints have supposedly been found in both Oklahoma and Wisconsin, however, details are not known by the author.

Big Feet

I know you thought that dinosaurs were getting huge and everything else stayed small, but the evidence shows that even the people were huge. Some may have stood 12 to 15 feet high and their footprints attest to that. Later we will find that this feature was found in other creations or hybrids.

New Mexico-1932 [Big humans]-In the great white sands a line of 13 prints were found imbedded in gypsum rock. Here is a strange part. The feet were 20 inches long.

Texas-Found in Glen Rose Texas, this Titan human footprint is 18 inches long. Another giant. [Below left]

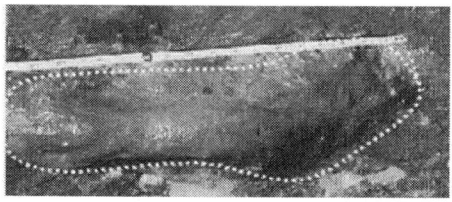 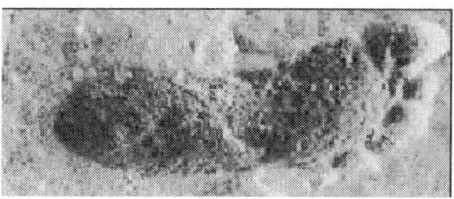

Kentucky 1896-This 14-½ inch human footprint impression [above right] was found embedded in rock. Estimated age of the rock was <u>Tertiary</u>.

Feet Around the World

These "Feet" haven't just been found in the United States. Here are a few other finds from around the world.

Turkey-Deposited in volcanic ash, the imprint below is estimated to be <u>Tertiary</u>, but could be much older.

Tanzania- There <u>Tertiary</u> human footprints were definitely made by humans years ago. Note the larger prints don't have the back and forth gate of the smaller "ape-like" footprints.

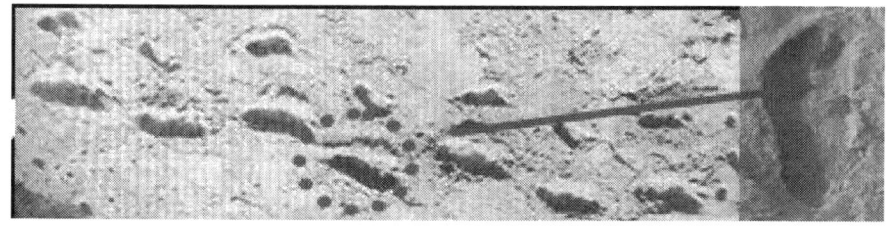

Australian Nephilim

Many Nephilimic footprints have been found in Australia.

- In 1969, 12 human footprints embedded in stone were found and estimated to be <u>Tertiary</u>.

- Embedded in sandstone beds on the Upper Macleay River, one print of foot was found with a toe 4 inches long and the total toe-span was 10 inches. The human would have been about 17 feet high.

- The largest Nephilim footprint found on the Blue Mountains must have belonged to a man 20 feet tall! As the width was well over 10 inches.

- A set of 3 huge footprints was discovered. The prints, each measured 2 foot long and 7 inches across the toes. A 6 foot stride was also apparent from the estimated 12 foot tall monster. These prints were preserved by volcanic lava and ash flows which dates them to be <u>tertiary</u> or older.

- In the Blue Mountains was found embedded in ironstone the deeply impressed print of a large human foot. The print was that of the instep, with all 5 toes clearly shown. This footprint measured 7 inches across the toes. The human making the print would have been about 12 foot tall.

Since the first finding of fossil impressions there have been over 90 hand and footprint impressions found. It has been estimated that the humans were over 14 feet tall by the size of the impressions. The footprints included those that were obviously children and full size adults with footprints 24 inches long by 12 inches wide across the toes. The handprints are similar with the largest about 16 inches between out stretched fingers. All prints have been dated to be <u>Tertiary</u>.

I'm sure that some of the Australian reports are duplicates, but there can be no mistake that many ancient Nephilimic humans roamed that Island nation.

Dinosaurs and Nephilim Together

Much evidence has been found showing even the early Trilobites were coexisting with the ancient humans. These trilobites probably died out before the beginning of the Cretaceous and men stepped on them before they became extinct. Just think about it! The strange part of this information is not that humans were here so long ago, but that they survived so very long through all types of disasters. Men and huge dinosaurs also walked together. Some scientists use that finding to prove that dinosaurs were here only 6 thousand years ago, but they mean that man was here long ago. Man didn't step on the huge dinosaurs as he had done to the trilobites, in fact, the humans might have been some ground cushion for the dinosaurs from time to time. Generally, they coexisted.

Shoeless Ancients

There has been a big deal put on the fact that these people were primitive in that many of the footprints do not show that people wore shoes and that is absurd as I discussed previously. Just think about how often you leave footprints. Where we find the footprints is usually along an area that was once a beach or along a muddy river. These people had shoes; they just didn't wear them in the water or on the beach.

Kentucky-1938--Three pairs of tracks [human] were sunk in gray sandstone [once a sandy beach during the <u>Cretaceous</u> period]. Photomicrograph studies showed that the tracks were not manufactured artificially or recently. See below left]

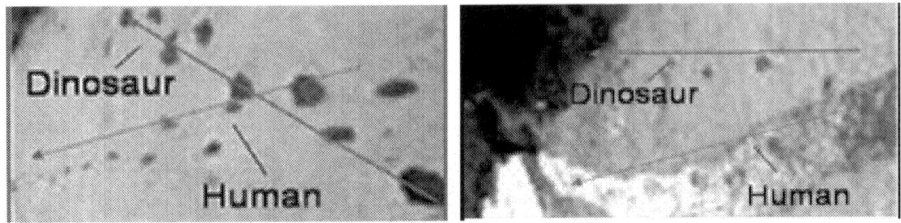

Texas Nephilim-In Paluxy, Texas we find Titan humans walking near dinosaurs was common. The example to the right is in a section that contains 14 human and 134 dinosaur tracks together. The Mud that had been under their feet turned to stone since the <u>Cretaceous.</u> [See next, top row]

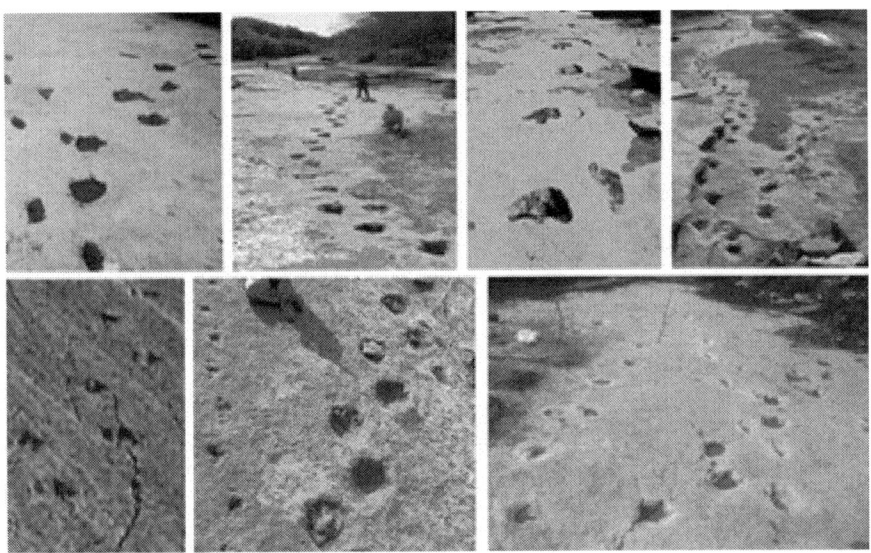

Texas Find of 1971-Another example from Glen Rose- man going one way and a dinosaur going the other. Lucky for the man and the footprint is huge 18 inches long. Its estimated age was <u>Cretaceous</u>. [See last image Preceding]

1976 Texas Close-up-Human and dinosaur prints were found together at Glen Rose, Texas. In one case, the dinosaur prints actually went over the top of one of the footprint impressions in a series. 203 dinosaur prints and 57 human prints were found in the same general area. The largest human print was over 16 inches long. Estimated age was <u>Cretaceous.</u> This one was found near the main group. The indication [right] is a famous human print taken from the area. Another footprint is shown left

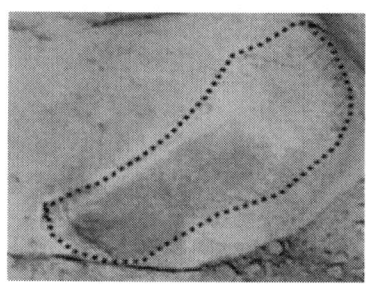 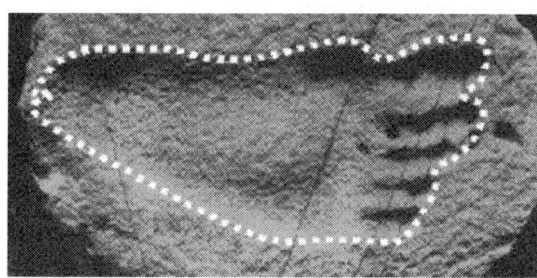

World Dinosaur Walks

Like the non-dinosaur footprints, North America wasn't the only place where dinosaurs and humans cohabitated. Here are a few of the many findings around the world.

Australian humans and dinosaurs-According to "Ancient Secrets of the Bible" human footprints commingled with <u>Cetaceous</u> dinosaur prints were found in Australia.

Russia-1983-According to the "Moscow News", human footprints were found alongside and in the same strata as three toed dinosaur tracks. The estimated age was <u>Cretaceous.</u>

Titan and Nephilim Bones in USA

Not only are there "footprints, but also the people themselves. Well, not the actual people, but the bones of these ancient people are still being found today. These are bones of people that looked just like we do today. The only difference is that they have been found in most unusual circumstances. A handprint and a fossilized finger are other unusual finds which show that these people were just like us. Even the find of human teeth indicates the existence of ancient humans all over the planet. Here are some examples of finds in the Unites States. Not only are these artifacts fossilized, but also many are located within materials which can be easily dated to a very ancient time.

Illinois-1962-A human skeleton was found 90 feet below the surface in a coal seam and was reported in "The Geologist". The estimated age was Cretaceous.

Bones in Shale-In the United States, the human bones shown below left, estimated to be Tertiary, were found inside shale.

 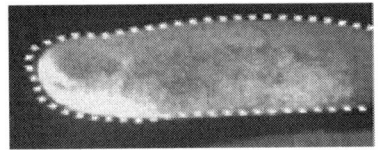

Another American find points to ancient humans-[sorry for the point comment]-The fossil above right is believed to be a finger found near dinosaur tracks. I have no idea how a finger fossil was made, but the fingernails look like modern man to be sure. X-rays of the stone finger shows dark areas where the bones would have been and widen areas around the "joints".

Nevada 1877-A human leg bone and knee were found sticking out of solid red quartzite rock. From the size of the leg section, the human was modern looking and was 12 feet tall. The estimated age of the stone formation was Cretaceous.

1853 Ohio- According to the "Zanesville Courier" the bones of a woman was found entombed in Sandstone. The impression of her body was remaining. Close to this discovery was a molded pair of hands similar to that shown next. The body was there when the sandstone formed during the Cretaceous.

Montana 1926- At the Number 3 Eagle Coal Mine, this human molar was found encased in Coal. It was estimated that the age that the coal was formed was Cretaceous.

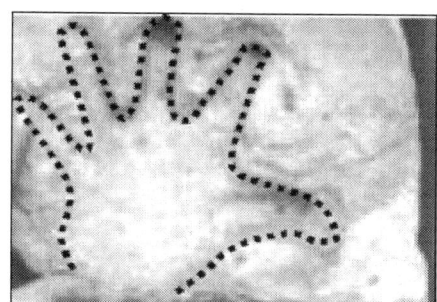 

Another Tooth- Still another modern human tooth has been found and this time it was in a core sample at a depth of over 4000 feet, inside a limestone deposit dated to be Cretaceous.

Colorado 1867- Human remains were found imbedded a silver vein at a depth of 400 feet. Estimated age that the vein was formed was during the Cretaceous Age. Another fossilized handprint was found in limestone. How it was made is a mystery and so is its age. It is estimated to be Cretaceous as well.

Pennsylvanian Coal mine - A possible huge skull bone fossil [above right] was found between anthracite veins in Pennsylvania, which were estimated to have formed in the Cretaceous Age. This particular skull fossil is twice as large as normal human skulls. Additional articles were found which included fossilized human bones embedded in Cretaceous coal. X-rays show the detail of the jaw portion of the fossil.

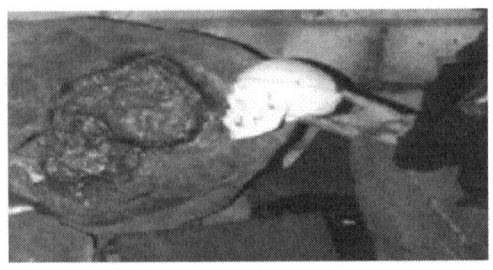

California 1866- A human skull was found. From fossils and shells wedged between portions of the skull, it was dated to be <u>Tertiary.</u>

California- An entire modern Homo Sapien skeleton was found and dated to be <u>Tertiary.</u>

Utah 1973- The lower halves of 2 modern looking human skeletons were found near a copper mine and estimated to be <u>Cretaceous</u> by Geologists.

Nephilim Around the World

Around the world, we find more of these amazing discoveries. Here are a few examples provided in many of the works listed in the bibliography.

Tanzania 1913- A modern human skull, no apelike brow ridge, was found cemented in rock. Estimated age of the rock was <u>Tertiary</u>. [See following left]

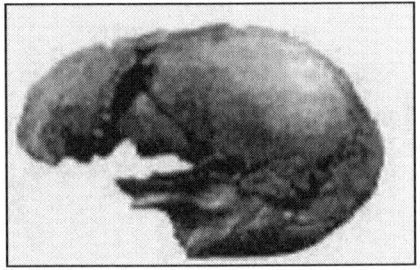
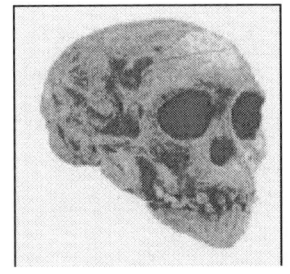

Africa-Tuang man/child- The drawing above right is of a skull, found in Africa is believed to be <u>Tertiary</u> and you can

48

see there are no heavy brows associated with primitive man and the chin is Homo Sapien-like. The canines are slightly larger than modern humans, but generally, this was a modern child.

W. Germany 1842-A poorly preserved human skull was found in brown coal. Pieces of the coal that were still embedded in the skull were estimated to be <u>Tertiary.</u>

Buenos Aires 1896-A very modern skull was found in a cave. Estimated age of the skull was Tertiary. Again, no heavy brow marks this as a "Normal" human skull. [See below left]

 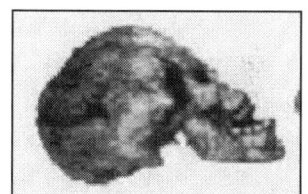

Italy 1860-A modern skull was found in Italy. Age of the skull was estimated to be Tertiary. Note the strong chin bone characteristic of modern man ---above right.

Italy 1958-A Modern human jawbone was found in a coal shaft at a depth of 600 feet- The estimated age of the coal was <u>Tertiary.</u> Try to pack 600 feet of coal in a few thousand years---It is simply impossible.

Guadeloupe Nephilim Skeletons

In the late 1700s, many human skeletons were excavated from this limestone. The limestone was situated 2-3 meters below a Tertiary coral reef so it is estimated to be Tertiary.

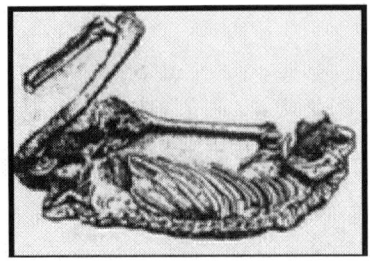 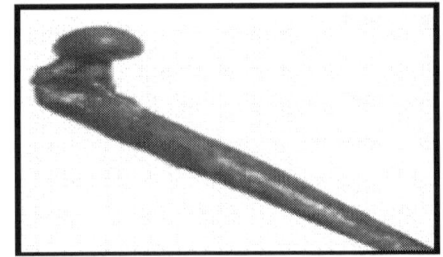

Above is a drawing left of one of the almost complete skeletons from Guadeloupe. The skeleton is not of a Homo Habilis or even Homo Erectus, it is of a normal Homo Sapien-Sapien human that lived before the coral reef had even started to form.

Green Nephilimic Skeletons

Sometimes the aging makes us better. Look at the fossilized human bone, above right. After tens of thousands of years, it has turned into Malachite. This process doesn't happen fast, so we can be sure that this was an ancient human as well. While you can't tell I the book, this bone has been turned to green malachite.

Intelligent Nephilim

It seems that the deeper people dig, the more we find out how very intelligent our ancestors were. Here are examples of building materials and even gold jewelry found in locations that have to be extremely ancient. This phenomenon again supports the theory that a very large number of humans lived on the Earth well before the time we used to believe was the dawn of mankind. Read the examples and see if you could possibly believe that these items were trapped inside coal and rock deposits as an aftermath of the worldwide flood, which some believe to have occurred less than 5 thousand years ago; especially considering that some of the deposits of coal are thousands of feet thick. As you go through this list, remember that the people finding these items could not have manufactured the results. In many of the cases, the information or artifacts were either witnessed by many or were actually part of the rock, coal, geode, or crystal in which they were found. Again, the details of the information can be found in books listed in the bibliography, but the overviews only are provided here to make the data easier to go through.

Smart Humans in North America

Nephilimic Artists-We should be able to gain some knowledge about a human by what he draws. In this area, what we might know is that they lived when the dinosaurs lived. There are many, many examples to choose from.

Utah Example-Here are ones from Utah and Arizona. Can you make out the drawings? I drew it in above the actual drawing on the one from Utah to help.

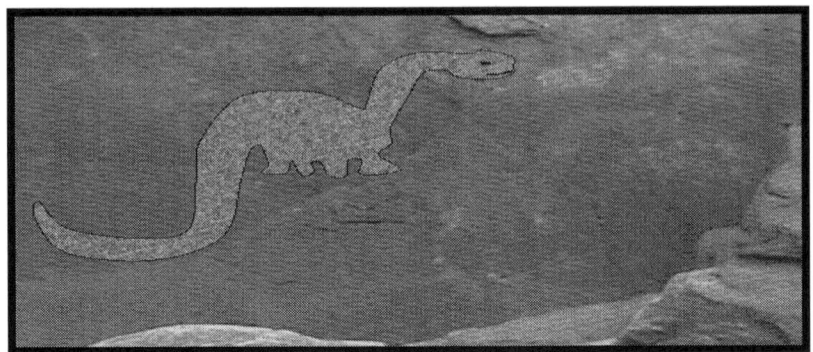

Arizona Example-In 1924 the Dohenny Scientific Expedition found Petroglyphs in the Havai Supai Canyon. Some of the pictures were of prehistoric beasts. One was of the Tyrannosaurus Rex extinct now many years. The pictures are fully patinated [a process of growing rust which typically takes many thousands of years], so the probability of recent artistry is extremely low.

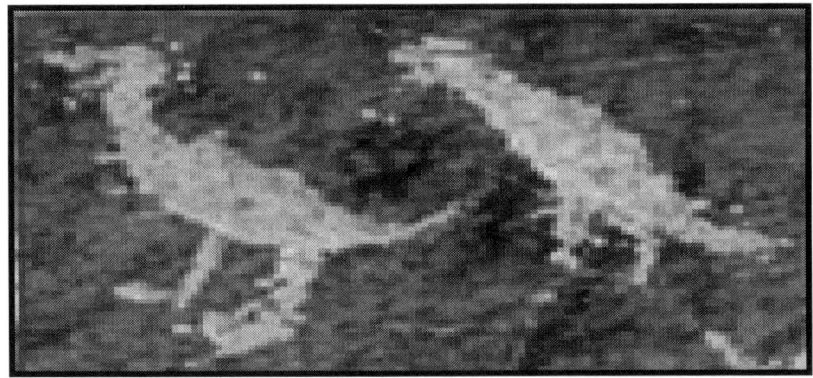

From these and many more of the drawings found there can be little doubt that ancient inhabitants of North America lived with the dinosaurs and had advanced to a fairly high level of society. That doesn't mean that dinosaurs lived here a thousand years ago, it means that people lived here during the Cretaceous. The crude artistry was not the only indicator of social advancement either. Here are a few more of the many examples that have been found.

Texas 1934-This graphic [left below] is of a hammer with partially coalified wooden handle that was found in Cretaceous Limestone. Here's the strange part. The Iron was processed such that it didn't rust.

 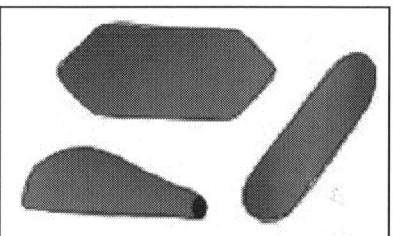

Pennsylvania-At the same site as was found the Cretaceous human bones embedded in coal, there was found a handle for some type of tool. The handle was coalified just like the sample from Texas.

Several Hundred wood pieces have been found that were worked by humans, but the thing that troubles many is that the wood was fossilized afterwards. General shapes are shown to the right above.

Oklahoma-1912-An iron cup was found inside a lump of coal. The estimated age of the coal was <u>Cretaceous.</u> [Look at the detail and workmanship from the graphic provided left]

West Virginia 1944- A "brass" bell with an iron clapper was found encased in a lump of coal. From the picture, right above, you can see that it was very similar to those manufactured today. The estimated age of the coal was Cretaceous.

Colorado about 1845-This time it was in the Marshal Coal bed some 300 feet below the surface. The "Scientific American" reported that, imbedded in a hollow place in a piece of coal was found a thimble. The coal beds were classed as lignitic. Apparently, the thimble was dropped sometime between the Tertiary and the Cretaceous period.

Colorado 1867-Tempered copper artifacts were found imbedded a silver vein at a depth of 400 feet. Estimated time that marked when the vein was formed was during the <u>Cretaceous period</u>.

Texas 1976- Another ancient Hammer was found alongside dinosaur prints. The composition of the hammer was 97% iron. The estimated age of the adjacent footprints was Cretaceous. [Just when did the Iron Age start anyway?]

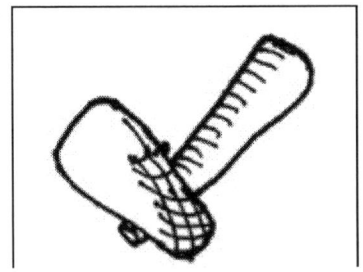 

Nevada 1869-The remains of a 2-inch long metal screw were found inside a block of feldspar. The calculated age of the stone was Tertiary. The screw itself was completely decomposed, but the rock contained a perfect mold of what had been inside.

Morrisonville, USA-1891- A 10-inch long, 8 carat gold chain was found encased in coal estimated to be Cretaceous.

Illinois 1851-At a depth of 120 feet a copper device like a boat hook came up during a well drilling. A "similar" one is shown.

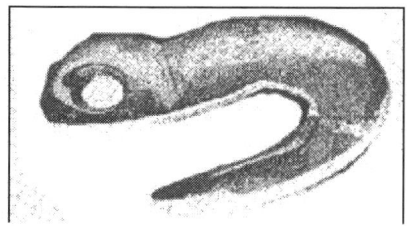 

California 1877-A metal Mortar and Pestle was found under some lava beds 300 feet deep. The mortar is about 4 inches in diameter. The estimated age of the objects was determined to be Early Tertiary.

Illinois 1851-While digging through rock, workers found the remains of 2 copper rings at a depth of 500 feet in the earth

Pennsylvania 1937 - A woman named Myrna Burdick found a spoon among ash from burnt coal. The ashes had not been disturbed after a large piece of coal was burned, but when they fell apart, the spoon was noticed among them.

Coin in Coal -A coin-like object embedded in a lump of carboniferous coal was found and was reported in "Strand Magazine" in 1901. The coal would have been Cretaceous. [No, there wasn't a date on the coin.]

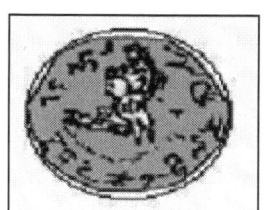 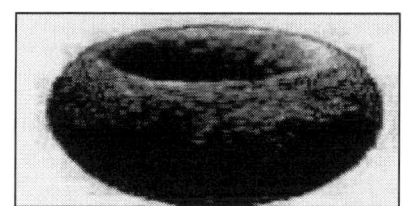

California 1866- Another stone mortar was found. From fossils and shells wedged between portions of a skull also found with it has been dated to be Tertiary.

1880 Colorado- According to the "American Antiquarian", inside a lump of coal, 300 feet deep, was found a perfectly formed thimble.

Ohio 1869- A slate wall was uncovered in a coal mine shaft at a depth of 100 feet. The wall was covered in strange letters. The letters were raised and well defined and the coal around the letters contained the impressions. Each letter was 3/4 inches long and arranged in lines of about 25 letters. The estimated age was Cretaceous.

Iowa-1897- A large stone [2x2x1feet] with multiple faces of an old man carved on it and a grid pattern on the remaining area was found 130 feet down in a coalmine. The estimated age was Cretaceous.

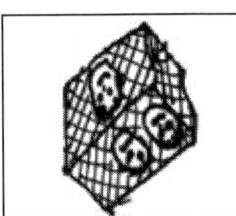 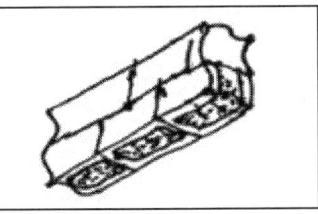 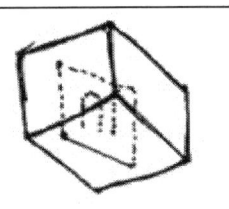

Oklahoma-1928- A block wall was found almost 2 miles deep in a coal mine. Each block was 12 x 12 x 12 inches polished on the outside and filled with gravel on the inside- There were multiple reports over 150 yard length of the same wall. The estimated age of the wall was Cretaceous.

Philadelphia 1829- A 30 cubic foot piece of marble was excavated from a depth of 60 feet. Inside the marble was a straight edged rectangular indentation. After a section of the marble was carefully removed, it was found that 2 distinct heavily engraved letters similar to an "I" and a "U" eleven inches long and 5.8 inches deep were on a square base. The estimated age was Cretaceous.

Strange Geodes

The old battery in a geode-The picture to the left below is some type of power conversion device found inside a geode, in California. Below the geode is a drawing of x-rays of the geode showing the elemental parts. These include a spring, core, plate, and electrical insulator. The same parts as you would expect in a battery. Maybe this is a new way to package batteries, but it takes a long time to complete the package. Both of the objects are extremely ancient and certainly, before we originally thought that everyone used electricity. The central metal core surrounded by the white material looks like a battery, although some even attribute the structure to that of a spark plug. Whatever it was, it was electrical. On the right is a drawing of the parts and a size comparison to a standard D-cell battery.

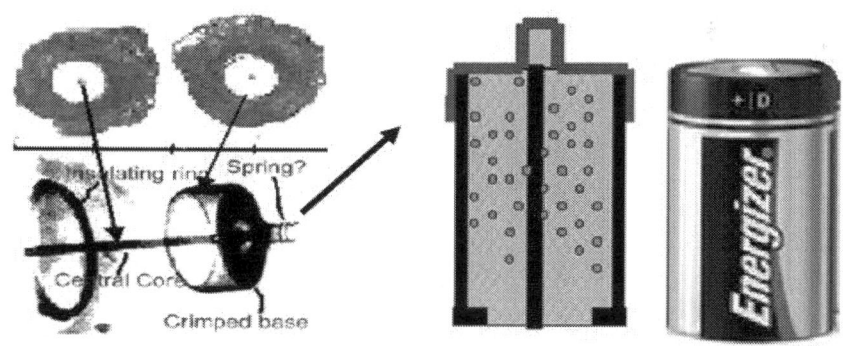

Another Geode

If that wasn't strange enough, still another geode was found with more goodies left behind by the ancient humans.

Geologist Mike Walters found this geode. Inside was a worked metallic bar or ring. This could only have been man-made.

California Find-Inside a Piece of Quartz crystal, a small metal piece was found it was obvious that it had been worked and was in the shape of a bucket handles.

California 1851-A cut iron nail was found inside a quartz crystal. Estimated age of the crystal was Tertiary. [Reported in the "Illinois Springfield Republican". It was very similar to those we use today as the sketch illustrates.

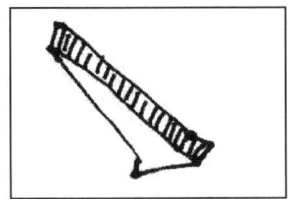

Amargosa Desert 1961- On the edge of the Desert was found a geode. Inside was found an iridescent stone with a 2mm x 17mm long metal rod. [You know Geodes must be old.]

Intelligence in Europe

The United States isn't the only place where these uncomfortable elements of evidence show up. Let's look at some from European sites.

1791 Germany-According to "The Fossils of South Down", inside a piece of flint was found an "Ancient Brass Pin".

France 1786-1788-Coins, tools and pieces of columns were brought up from areas below 11 different beds of limestone, which were estimated to be Early Tertiary.

France, 1862-Man-made chalk balls were found near Leon and were estimated to be Early Tertiary. The balls were almost perfectly round and could not have been naturally produced.

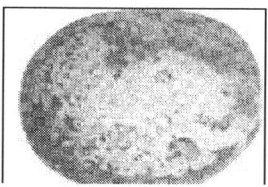 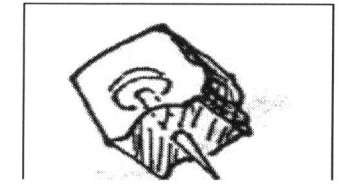

Britain-1844-The head of a metal nail was found encased in a 9-inch thick block, similar to the illustration, much of the nail was lost to corrosion and the block was dated to be Cretaceous.

UK-1844-Gold thread was found imbedded in stone estimated to be Cretaceous. The discovery was reported in "The Times".

1844- Scotland-A nail half embedded into a granite block was excavated from the Kingoodie Quarry near Dundee in Scotland. The granite was estimated to be Cretaceous. The point of the nail was found projecting about half an inch (quite eaten with rust) into the 'till', the rest of the nail lying along the surface of the stone to within an inch of the head, which went right down into the body of the stone.

1874 England -Several shells were found which were engraved with faces, but the strange part was that they were determined to be Tertiary.

1872 England--Drilled sharks teeth were found which were determined to be Tertiary. The teeth had perfectly round holes probably were used as necklace beads.

Germany 1886-An Iron Cube was found 2.6 x 2.6 x 1.9 inches. 4 sides were flat and the other 2 were convexed with groves incised around the flat sides. The estimated age of the object was Early Tertiary.

Intelligence in Africa-Africa gets into the act with some of the most amazing articles. These are some of the more famous of the Ancient Human, manufactured elements. In South Africa in the 1970s over 200 "1 to 4" inch iron spheres were found. Some were cored with a spongy material inside. Some were formed with fine grooves etched into the circumference. The spheres were found in beds of Pyrophyllite with an estimated age of Cretaceous or earlier. Look at the fine detail of the one shown below left. It was not "naturally" formed.

Now for Something Really Strange

The fact that ANY artifacts could have survived over a million years is unbelievable and almost all of the artifacts were destroyed over time, but some remain showing that these people know about things we are just now learning. Now I'm going to bring up something that will sound like an absurdity. These people could grow rocks. The preceding items show that ancient humans were somewhat civilized, but you would have to believe that they would have left things that are more amazing if there civilization existed for over 100 thousand years. Well, proof may be hard to come by. Anything made of metal is probably long gone, but we don't have to rely on metal for the rock study. We may have amazing evidence in the form of blocks that grew into a wall or a floor. I know it's hard to believe and it sounds comical, but it's apparently true.

Block Growing

Block Growing by Ancient Humans was evident in the remains of their buildings. Apparently, the central core of the blocks was not as hardened as the outside rings. Layer after layer built up until the desired form was met. The shapes fit together so closely that the block must have been grown in place rather than moved to a sight fully manufactured. The picture next has been determined to be a floor section millions of years old. The central core is almost completely gone, but the outside lattice structure of this ancient floor can still be seen.

W. Virginia-This waffle pattern has been found on the ground and the blocks have been estimated to be Cretaceous. One thought is that it represents the pattern on the skin of a giant reptile. The joints between each waffle pattern can be easily seen today. Each of the blocks is layered as though the blocks had been grown in place rather than being quarried at a distant sight.

In the close-up shown, note how close together each of the blocks is positioned to adjacent ones. Not even a needle could pass between their interfaces. The interior of each of the floor stones was of a softer material and eventually was eaten away .

Something possibly even more amazing is that the block growing technique was known for many thousands of years. The picture below is of a wall estimated to be thousands of years old and the blocks are still in good shape. Both samples were found at sites in the United States, which must have been a very popular place to live during very ancient times. We're going to revisit this whole idea of block growing in the next book, but it should be recognized that during the very ancient times, humans knew things we are just learning about today.

Oklahoma

The "Grown blocks" in this Oklahoma Wall shown, were believed to have been part of an ancient Phoenician metalworking plant, but they could have been and probably were much older.

Here is a question----If the blocks were not grown in place, where did the people find these perfectly matching stones that have not been externally shaped. We can tell the stones were not worked because the outer layer of ringed material on each block has not been violated.

Peruvian Grown Blocks

The same capability is evidenced around the world. In Peru, we find a strange grid pattern trail. The grid pattern with no space between blocks looks mighty familiar. Some indicate that these thousands and thousands of holes were engraved into the pathway, but the holes make a terrible road, and would have been an almost impossible accomplish even if there was a purpose for them. Before the insides wore away, the path would have been a very nice roadway.

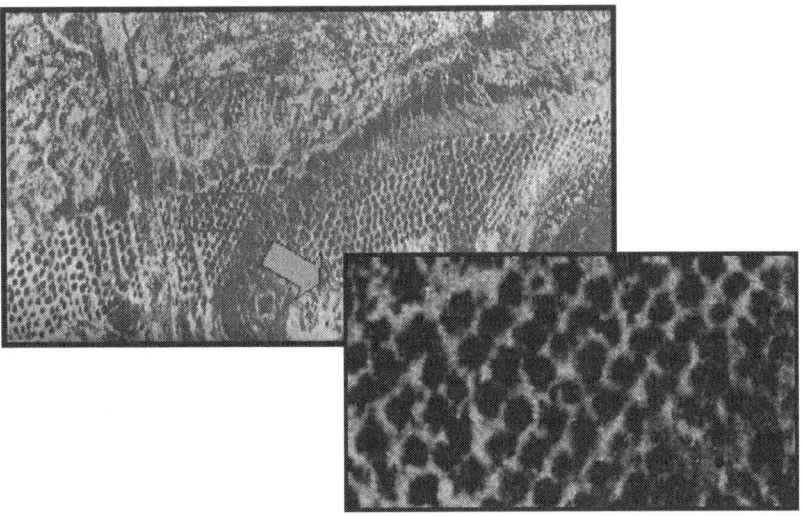

More Peruvian Blocks

A road with thousands of holes isn't the only evidence in Peru. What about stones with a bubble of air inside them? What about eleven of them on the same type structure. These blocks were not found on the ground with air in their middle, so what else could have been done? Notice something else in the example below. The inside cavity does not have the same shape as the outside. This suggests that the outside surface characteristics were determined by some type of mold that "forced" the desired shape. This also suggests that the block was grown in place just like all the others mentioned in this section. Here is still another observation to make. The inside of the blocks are neither smooth nor do they fit tightly together as the outside does. It is as if there was a mold only around the outside of the block to restrict growth.

Australian Grown Blocks

Researcher, David Cambell, who initiated the research into the examples of "Grown blocks" in North America also indicated that similar structures have been found in Australia. Some believe the "grown" blocks there are just natural phenomenon that, somehow, were stacked neatly into a wall, but their close fit, regular features strongly suggest that they could not be natural structures. Below is a similar "grown" block from a wall in Australia. It was a neat trick. Maybe we will remember how to grow a building in the near future, but one this is certain. The ancient Nephilim new many things we do not.

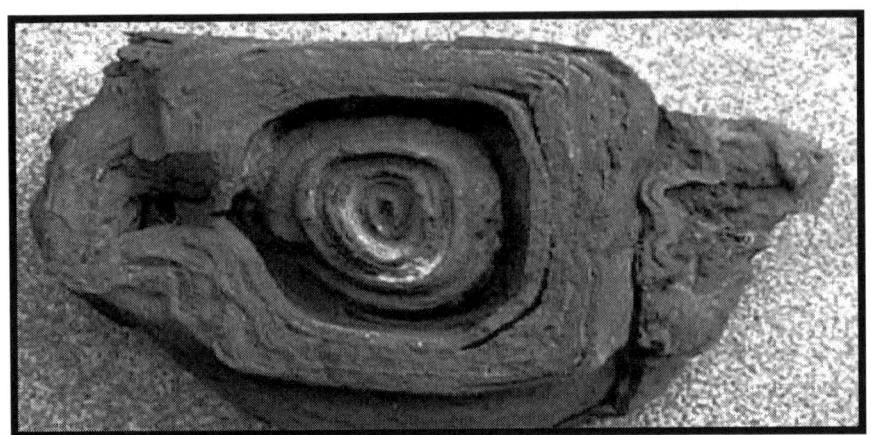

Note how the block appears to have been "grown" in layers until the outside dimensions would have completely fit next to an adjacent block. Possibly a portion of a second block is shown on the right side of the one depicted.

I know you have never heard of a concept like growing blocks, but the evidence is clear and the resulting "grown blocks" were very strong to last these thousands of years. Similar blocks have been found in North America, South America, Australia, Babylonia, and Egypt. The images below are of the largest building blocks ever used and the center one shows there was no space between irregular block shapes. These are found in Russian, Peru, and Lebanon [Left to right] No one knows how old, how they were made, and who made them. A tiny person is standing by each to show size.

This evidence suggests that these ancient humans, who probably included our Lilith character, knew things we have not yet relearned and he lived all over the world. One of the many capabilities enjoyed by these ancient ones was Genetic Manipulation.

Lilith Made Homo-Habilis

Certainly we don't know the names, but Nephilimic Humans were very advanced and the evidence is clear. These ancient humans manipulated the genetics of the animals including the ape animals to finally produce the Homo-Habilis [Ape-man]. He could walk on two legs and carry things for the humans, but he evidently was very difficult to domestic or when he was tamed, he could not perform the tasks that the humans wanted him to do.

Below are a few descriptions from ancient texts around the world the examples are from Africa, the Middle East, the Far East, and the Americas. It was pretty much known by everyone in ancient times. The stories have been romanticized a little over time, but I think you can see the detail.

Ngombe Tribe Description

In Africa, the same story was told. Hairy men became human after coming in contact with Nephilim-like humans. According to Ngombe tribe folklore, we find the following:

A sky person [Nephilim/Lilith] saw a hairy man [Homo-Habilis]. She married him and removed his hair [Homo-Erectus]. Then a Garden was made for man to live in."

The offspring of this union was less animal like just like all the other descriptions.

Rhodesian Description

The stories from the Wahungwe tribe of Rhodesia seemed to infer that there was a continual genetic manipulation study going on with the 6th day man. After some time, the "man" could have offspring with Nephilim and the offspring evidently could procreate on their own and the Nephilim didn't have to continue to inbreed with the humans.

The first night Mwueti [probably Ape man] touched Morongo [probably a Nephilim named Lilith] . Each night she gave birth to different animals [genetic manipulation produced the Homo-Africansis and Robustus ape-men {like the famous Lucy}]. Finally she had regular children [possibly Homo-Habilis]. After that, Mwueti had sex with his daughters [the Homo-Erectus was finally able to procreate] and the human race was formed.

India Creation Myth

The first humans were covered with thick hair, but when they mated they produced people as they are now.

You guessed it the hair was gone after Lilith mated with them.

Sumerian Gilgamesh Story

Aruru [God] pinched off some clay and created a [primitive man] Enkidu-his whole body was covered in hair. [This would most likely be the Homo-Habilis ape-man]

He knew neither people nor country, with cattle, he quenched his thirst, a hunter and brigand—Shamhat [one of the Annunaki- Nephilim counterparts] must take off her clothes and reveal her attractions. Do for the primitive man, as women [Nephilim] do. [Shamhat was certainly the Lilith character.] She pulled not away, Enkidu was aroused.

---Afterward- the gazelles saw Enkidu and scattered, for Enkidu had stripped--- his body was too clean [The hair was all gone. His offspring were possibly Homo-Erectus humans].

His legs were diminished-he could not run as before, he had become wiser—Enkidu, you have become like a god [Nephilim]- He shall bring up daughters of gods [hybrid man].

This is the most descriptive and shows that there were female Nephilim [Lilith#1] that had sex with male Homo-Habilis and homo-erectus. They sort of forced themselves to sleep with this lowly creature, but the union did produce viable offspring.

Another Sumerian Story

According to "The Epic of Creation (*Enuma Elish*)" the Sumerians tell about the same story.

The first children of the gods were the Lahmu - 'the hairy ones'. [This is probably talking about the Homo-Habilis.]

Aruru on the direction of Ea, mixed clay with the blood of one of the other gods to make seven men and seven women to bear the workload of the Iggigi. [This indicates that the 6th day man was created to be a worker for the Iggigi & Anunnaki "Nephilim".]

Later, under the direction of Marduk, mankind was created. [This shows that the modern Adamic man was created later.]

Babylonian History of Man

From "*Atra Hasis*"-This comes from a text called the Atra Hasis that was found along with the Sumerian creation story reference in other sections.

When the gods instead of man did the work, they bore the loads. The gods' load was too great, the work was too hard, the trouble was too much, the great Anunnaki made the Igigi carry the workload sevenfold. [Nephilim groups had to do their own work before the invention of Homo-Habilis.]

Let the womb-goddess create offspring, and let man bear the load of the gods!" [Experiments to make Homo-Habilis] They asked the womb-goddess [Lilith] to create man to do their work.

Later we find in other pre-Babylonian works that the hair of the offspring from a union between this womb-goddess and an ape-man fell off. This identifies the change from Homo-Habilis ape-man to Homo-Erectus man.

Mandaeans of Iran Story

According to their traditions, we find the following:

The gods first made man, When he was finished, he looked like a man, but moved on all fours [Homo-Robustus and Africansis] He had the face of an ape, and made noises like a sheep. [The Hairy Homo-Habilis] Only later did he put in a soul and teach him and make him erect.

This is also the conversion of ape-man to homo-Erectus. The sex part with Lilith was softened, but the similarity is clear.

Tibetan History of Man

From "The Monkey and the Rock Ogres"

The Ogres were a race of devils [Possibly this means that Nephilim were on the Earth before man.]

One of the females became smitten with lust with a monkey. [One of the female Nephilim {Lilith} procreated with an ape-man to make a new type of ape-man {Homo-Habilis}.]

The two were united as husband and wife and she bore 6 monkey children. [The Nephilim inbred with ape-men. <u>Lilith was sort of the mother of mankind</u>.]

Some of the children were misshapen, loathsome, stupid and vulgar. [Some of the offspring were monsters and giants as described many places.]

Some of them were endowed with wisdom, patience, virtue and sensitivity. [Some of the hybrid-men were the great men of old as described in the 6th chapter of Genesis.]

The children lived in the forest of Assembled Birds and they had insatiable appetites. [A reference to the giants eating everything around as described before.]

After three years, they had eaten all of the food that was available and God sprinkled seed to fill the garden with crops that required no cultivation [The Garden of Eden story, sort-of]

The monkey-children' hair and tails grew shorter. They then learned to speak and became human. [The hybrids were no longer ape-like. This sounds like the transformation to Homo-Erectus.]

American Confirmation

In the Americas, the same story was told. *"Men were once hairy and monkey like."* Something happened to them and I think you know what it was. It had to do with Nephilim, Lilith, and sex.

Inca legends

The age of primitive man, [hairy Homo-Habilis] was before the age of heroes [Nephilim and demigods]

Primitive "hairy", Homo-Habilis, man turned into heroes probably by a process called breeding with Lilith.

Aztec and Mayan history

According to Codex "Laticano-Vatino", we again find elements of an identical history.

During the age of the four winds men turned into monkeys.

Homo-Habilis was most likely very hairy. While this is backwards, Lilith was the instigator.

Habilis Becomes Erectus

If these early people could grow blocks, the genetic manipulation should be a reasonable capability for these ancient ones to have. For the sake of this study, let's assume that the change from Homo-Habilis to Homo-Erectus appears to be a genetic manipulation by these ancient humans. The

Bible indicates God came down, saw Homo-Habilis and created a new man on the 6th Day without the help of Lilith or the Nephilim. Ancient texts tell us a strange story that is confirmed in many texts from around the world.

"The ancient ones wanted servants and tried to make them. By modifying traits, a "better" human was produced, but this new "human" still wasn't what the ancient humans thought they wanted, so they took more drastic measures." Similar writings are found by the ancient Aztecs, Sumerians, Jews, and around the world. It certainly was believed that humans were initially "created" to be the servants of the master race. We will look at some of these texts and stories in a minute, but let's also look at the Homo-Erectus as the real beginning of mankind. Lilith #1 was supposed to be the "developer of Ape to Homo-Habilis.

Erectus & the 6th Day Man

The ancient texts may also tell us about the major change from the Homo-Habilis ape-man to Homo-Erectus Human. One of the major descriptions of this change can be found in our Bible as it refers to the creation of the 6th day human. While the book of Genesis doesn't go into much detail concerning the "creation" other works from around the world strongly suggest that the animal characteristics of the pre-6th day humans and the after 6th day humans were substantially different. We will look at some of those references as well. Speaking of different. I get so frustrated at people trying to translate out the words Us and They from Genesis rather than just reading it and knowing that "people make and God Creates".

Nephilim Modify Proconsul to Homo Habilis

> ***Genesis 1:26*** *And the elohiem [Nephilim led by biogenetic Scientist, Lilith] said, Let **us** make man in **our** image, after **our** likeness:*
>
> <u>The Creator God Make Homo Erectus</u>
>
> ***Genesis 1:27-*** *Then [the creator]God **created** man in **his** own image, in the **image of God** created **he** him; male and female created **he** them.*

If you get nothing else from this book please see that these two verses are completely different. Moses put in the plural pronouns on purpose and he converted the word make to Create in the second verse to make sure no one would get these confused.

I'm not making these things up, they just seem weird to us because we have not been introduced to these possibilities as of yet. If you bear with me a little longer, I think it will become clearer. Remember that these ancient stories have been told and retold over the centuries and there is a bit of fantasy that has been introduced, but the core information should not be ignored especially as it is verified by science and archeological evidence.

The Sixth Day Creation

Now we are coming to the thing I call the 2nd creation. The early, early "men" / Nephilim, were lazy. They had been trying to manipulate, breed, and modify the animals to help them in their everyday lives. The finest result was the Homo-Habilis ape-man. God stepped in to change him to the Homo Erectus man. Homo Erectus still wasn't good enough for the Nephilim would-be rulers of the Earth. The Lilith scientists stepped in again to produce all types of humans that were colonize all over the world.

Nephilim/Lilith Wanted a Servant

The Nephilim had to do WORK! It was no fun doing all the work; even if some of the work was to create monsters and different creatures and other fun things.

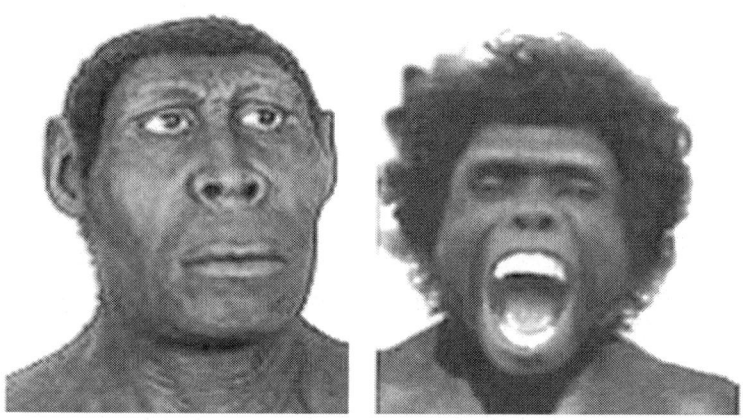

These Nephilim felt that they needed to make a new "man" to do the work and worship them [sort of like a dog worshiping his master], but they were not having much success because most of the creatures shown above could not be domesticated. Why should they have to do work anyway? Some believe that God probably felt compassion for the Nephilim and made them a worker. Others believe that it was the work of a particular Nephilim named Lilith. My belief is that it was a little of both. The Nephilimic humans could manipulate genetics, but the ancient Jewish texts indicate that they did not understand the ramifications or complexity of what they were doing. Below is a segment of a book found with the Dead Sea scrolls typically called the "Book of Secrets". After each verse, I have added comments in bold to amplify its meaning to this subject.

Those who would penetrate the origins of knowledge, along with those who hold fast to the wonderful mysteries (of magic;) [This is referring to Nephilim-Lililths, and humans that practice the secrets of "magic". The magic we are discussing here would be genetic magic]

--those who walk in simplicity as well as those who are devious in every activity of the deeds of humanity; those with a stiff neck, and all the mass of the Gentiles, [All humans including those that were not pure blood Adamic humans were not left out of this warning.]

--with (this I beseech your attention. All of the) secrets of sin (and magic were known in the past) but they [preflood humanoids] did not know the secret of the way things are nor did they understand the things of old. [No one knew the ramifications of meddling with nature before the flood.]

They did not know what would come upon them, so they did not rescue themselves without the secret of the way things are. [Magic did not warn or save Nephilim, like Lilith, or Adamic humans from the flood.]

It is true that all the peoples reject evil, yet it advances in all of them. Who wants his money to be stolen by a wicked man, but where is the person that has not robbed the wealth of another? [No humanoid can escape evil. Even if he thinks that he is doing good, it can change to evil.]

What shall we call man who will call no one on earth wise or righteous? It is not a human possession (to act on wisdom.) It is not (possible because) wisdom is hidden except for the wisdom of cunning evil, and the schemes of Belial (who modified creation,) a thing that ought never to be done again, except by the command of his Maker. [Only God has the wisdom to modify creation. Belial (possibly a term for Lilith) modified creation and it should NEVER be done again.]

(God controls) every secret, and he limits every deed and what (magic that is known by) the Gentiles, for He created them and their deeds also [The magic that is done by the non-Adamic humanoids is "allowed" by God. None is accomplished without his knowing. To me this is saying God could have guided Lilith in the manufacture of the 6th day human, could have done it him self.]

Consider the soothsayers, those teachers of sin and (magic. Do not regard) your foolishness, for the vision is sealed up from you, and you have not properly understood the eternal mysteries. [Manipulation of nature and Magic cannot be understood by man or Nephilimic human. It is foolish to try to use them for good.]

You have not become wise in understanding (my secrets); for you have not properly understood the origin of Wisdom.

This is the most important verse. In order to understand how to manipulate nature in a good way, you must understand how it came into being, which you cannot.

Homo Erectus or Sixth Day Man

Let's look a little closer at the differences between the Homo-Habilis and the Homo-Erectus human. There was a big jump in "evolution" between the animal called Homo-Habilis and this new creature. The Habilis could sort-of walk on 2 feet, but he would not have been a good worker.

Erectus, on the other hand was, very much like a normal human. His skull is shown next left. The nose, jaw, brain cavity and other elements had changed almost overnight. He now was a human.

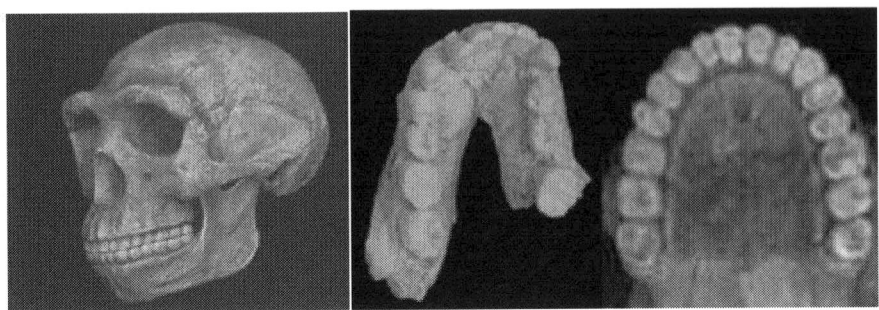

The Nephilim had gone about as far as they could with apes in the Habilis structure and they needed help.

The Habilis <u>didn't even have an opposing thumb</u>. He <u>didn't have the powerful neck muscles</u>, or the <u>large occipital opening at the base of the skull</u>. His <u>feet were still hand-like</u> and his <u>thigh bones were curved like other apes</u> and <u>his brain was still half the size of the Erectus</u>. Then, all of a sudden-- humans changed.

Even his jaw was greatly different. Notice how narrow the jaw-line was on the Habilis [previous middle] when compared to the Erectus human [previous right].

Homo-Erectus, on the other hand, was the first true human of this line. His features were man-like including his teeth, pelvis, and legs. He was much larger than the 3.5 foot tall Habilis and his brain had swelled to over 800 cubic centimeters or almost twice that of his very recent predecessor. All of a sudden, this new creature was using tools like the one shown. Those things didn't happen by chance and they all point to a very strong, very articulate, very manlike worker.

After the Nephilim helped engineer this new creature, they immediately began griping again. I'm sure that the man that was created was a good worker, because his bone structure and articulation level tell us that, but the Nephilim now wanted something different. They wanted to be worshipped like gods and this new creature was not worshipping the Nephilim like they expected and he was not much of a free thinker. The Nephilim actually thought they wanted smarter humans. They felt they needed a smarter human for three reasons.

- *According to the ancient texts, the first reason was so that they could do even more of the work,*

- *the second reason was so that the creatures would worship them,*

- *And the third reason, sort of in the back of their minds, was so that they could become the expendable part of an army to eventually defeat God in another battle with heaven. [The Nephilim, including Lilith, seemed to always try to take over heaven according to the ancient Jewish texts.]*

All this sex with the Nephilim to create a better human, spawned the Lilith story/history. The beginning of the discussions of Lilith seemed to come from the ancient Jewish community, but they weren't the only ones.

World View of Homo-Erectus

The Jews weren't the only group that had a similar realization of the creation path. Let's look at an overview of stories relating to the creation of this new man from around the world before turning to the Mediterranean area and looking for Biblical similarity and enhancements.

See how very similar the creation stories are even with the vast separation between people of the ancient times. Surviving writings are not as prevalent in the Americas, so the details and comparisons are somewhat limited, but the stories certainly are the same, as we will see. Some of the details may not make too much sense right now but they will as later descriptions paint a complete picture of not only the six day creation, but what followed. This collection comes from South America, Central America, North America, The Far East, Africa, and the Middle East. Not too many places have been left out, so how can we leave this timeline out of our "Normal History" classes? Here are some things to look for.

- *God remade man [indicating that there were several "Creations" of humans]*
- *The new man was very primitive and many times depicted as hairy or monkey-like. [Homo Habilis]*
- *The new man would not worship god*
- *The new man mixed with the Nephilim [essentially the Lilith character] and the hair fell off and the man became*

smarter. *[The new man with his hair fallen off is shown above. Sometimes called Homo-Erectus]*

Incan History of Man

This history comes from Peru and the Inca. The time line of this history has been slightly changed because it was a little backwards from all others and was believed to have been copied in an incorrect order. According to several historians, this is the more correct time-line.

A Golden ship came from the stars. In the ship was a female named Oryana [possibly the Lilith character]. She was to be the mother of earth.

The god/goddess Oryana had 4 webbed fingers on each hand. She gave birth to 70 earth children. Then she went back to the stars.

The god re-made man. This time he endowed each man with his own language and brought him to life with his divine breath. [The story of the creation of man on the 6th day. Notice that this was considered the RE-Make of man]

He sent the giants among primitive man [Nephilim inbred with this primitive man]

Giant tunnels were built by the ancient race of white men to protect them from endless cataclysms [possibly to protect against a very ancient war]

The sons and daughters of the sun instructed them in a manner of knowledge including-language, customs, and art [Nephilim taught this new man everything]

Viracocha [one of the Nephilim] and his disciples could walk on water [Levitation was known similar to that described in the Bible as both Peter and Jesus walked over the water]

A great flood was sent to destroy the giants. All perished except one man and one woman. [The Noah story and the worldwide flood]

After the massive flood, Viracocha descended to the Earth and shaped animals [Nephilim reintroduced animals after the flood]

"After people arrived at Tulan and before going west, our language was the same. Our speech became different—alas we have abandoned our speech." [Tower of Babel Story]

Viracocha flew some of the people to other parts of the world [Tower of Babel story- mankind is scattered over the world.]

The sons of the sun left the people [Finally the Nephilim and their offspring died off or left?]

Mayan History of Man

From " Popol Vuh [Book of Counsel]"

After many wars and fighting, God separated the sky and the Earth, [Something terrible happened to the earth during the ancient wars]

Then he made trees [Trees were created before animals]

Then animals were created, but the animals did not praise him [Animals were created before man]

God fashioned humans in hopes that they would worship him, but they were made out of mud and dissolved. [Ape-man was created but he would not serve the Nephilim humans.]

Then "he" made more humans out of wood [The Nephilimic humans made hybrids by genetic manipulation].

They looked like real people, but did not praise god because they had no memory and learned too much [This new human looked different than the earlier creatures. They were more like the Nephilim. The Nephilim taught this man too much about the worldly things]—

An imposter named Vukub-Cakix and his giant sons challenged the Gods [One of the Nephilim tried to take over heaven, just like the Satan story of the Bible.]

God wreaked revenge by turning the world upside down. [There is no direct mention of this in our Bible, but geologic history shows that the Earth axis has flipped many times as suggested here.]

Then God re-made man from maize. [The Adamic human was made.]

This time he limited man's understanding of the world. [The Jewish version says, God told man to stay away from the tree of knowledge.]

They finally praised God and light spread over the world. [Unlike the predecessor humans, these Adamic humans worshiped God.]

Aztec History of Man

From "Five Creations of Man"

In the first creation, giants walked the Earth. [Nephilimic humans were created before man. Many texts including the Bible speak of the Nephilim as being giants.]

After a battle, the giants were knocked into the water and the Earth was consumed by jaguars [After a terrible war between heaven and the Nephilim, the Nephilim were banished to Earth.]

In the Second creation, the leader of the giants had another battle and took control. [The Nephilimic Humans became the rulers of the world.]

During the second creation, people turn into monkeys and the world was destroyed by wind. [The Nephilim inbred with primitive man and the monkey-like Homo-Habilis seems to have been the outcome.]

In the third period, the world was governed by the rain god and destroyed by a fiery rain sent by the creator. [This seems to be a reference to the affects of huge "fiery rain meteors" that hit the earth about 13 thousand years ago according to many historians including the ancient Jewish texts. In their wake, Jewish texts tell us that 1/3 of the world's population was destroyed.]

In the fourth creation, the world was ruled by the water goddess. It was ended by a great flood and everyone turned into fishes- [Like the Biblical story, Adamic man was made and the great flood covered the world.]

In the fifth creation, God remade man, but the Earth remained in darkness until the sun was recreated [This is possibly a somewhat twisted reference to the survivors of the flood and the coming of the sun/son of God.]

Navaho History of Man

Navaho and Apache Indian Legends

In the first beginning men came to the top surface of the world [Some Nephilimic humans survived a terrible war which forced them underground. There is much evidence of humans having to live under ground to survive.]

In the second beginning which was called the animal-hero Age. The Earth was set in order [This seems to be saying that everything was remade including the ape-man.]

In the third beginning, called the God Age- God slayed the monsters [I believe this is saying that Nephilim mixed with humans. Their offspring turned into Giants and monsters according to many, many texts, especially Jewish texts. God eventually destroyed the strange hybrids.]

In the fourth beginning the Navaho were created [After the worldwide flood, man replenished the world again.]

Creek Indian History of Man

Creek Indian Legends

First god created giants before man. [Reference to the Nephilimic humans before normal humans.]

The giants became cannibals. [Some texts tell of the offspring of the Nephilim eating people. One reference is the "Book of Giants" found among the Dead Sea Scrolls.]

They were destroyed by flood. [All the offspring were killed in the flood.]

Only a few people were saved from the flood.

African Bantu History of Man

The Creator made the world

Then he made man out of clay [This, evidently was the Nephilimic human.]

Man turned out to be a lizard [This whole concept of reptile-like humans keeps occurring in ancient texts. Evidently, these were real humanoids. If you remember the "serpent" being in the Garden of Eden, it doesn't seem too difficult to imagine.]

God put him in the ocean for 5 days

On the 6th day, he was still a lizard [Just like the Jewish History a man was created on the 6th day. This 6th day man came next but he was not completely like man of today.]

After getting back in the water, he became a man on the 8th day. [Just like in the Biblical story, Adam was created after he rested on the 7th day. The eighth day man was the Adamic man according to the Bible and the Bantu.]

African Ngombe History of Man

People before men lived in the sky [The Nephilim lived on Earth and on other planets. There is much evidence to suggest this probability.]

A magnificent Garden was made for man [This would have been a Garden of Eden before the Adam and Eve version.]

A female saw a hairy man in the forest [Nephilim {Lilith} inbred with primitive Homo-Habilis.]

She married him and removed his hair. [The hybrid man, Homo-Erectus, was created.]

The evil Ebenga, a serpent god, tempted/seduced the woman [Eve seduced by the serpent story with the second Lilith personification being Ebenga.]

Afterwards, her child brought witchcraft and misery into the world [The Biblical Cain story.]

Chinese History of Man

The Chuang-Tzu text from China contains a great description of this hard working servant. He seemed to always have a smile no matter what type of workload he was given. You would think that the Nephilim would love this worker, but it continues to indicate that the new man would not speak to the Nephilim and not worship them.

They appeared to smile as if pleased. Absent minded they kept forgetting speech.

They behaved as though wanting in themselves, but without looking up to others [did not worship the Nephilim]

In that which was One, they were of god; in that which was not One, they were man.

And so between man and the divine no conflict ensued.

This was not to be a true man.

[The offspring depicted here was evidently half human half Nephilim/god. Sort of Lilith's offspring. Afterwards, a true man, generally called Adamic man, was created according to this document.]

"Hypostasis of the Angels" *Come let us [rulers of the world] make a man that will be soil from the Earth. They modeled the creature as wholly of the Earth. Now the rulers [also] made the body of a female with the face of a beast [Possibly describing Lilith].—and he breathed into his face and the man came to have a soul and remained on the ground—the spirit saw the soul-endowed man upon the ground and the spirit descended and came to dwell within him and that man became a living soul.*

"Les Questions de Jean"-*And he [one of the Nephilim] imagined in order to make man for his own service, [Just as we have been reading, the Nephilim needed servants and old 6th day man was going to be that servant.]and took the lime of the earth and made man in his semblance. And he ordered* *the angel of the 2nd heaven to enter the body of lime; [Although the man from dirt is similar, the description of 6th day man being part angel is not a common thought. Instead of a 2nd heaven angel, most indicate that this was Lilith.]and he took another part and made another body in the form of a woman, and he ordered the angel of the 1st heaven to enter therein. [We can tell this isn't the Adam and Eve story as the woman was made from dirt rather than a rib.]The angels cried exceedingly on seeing themselves covered in distinct forms by this mortal envelopment.*

This may show that when heavenly creatures gain physical bodies they could not go back to heaven. That would make them sad. It also might mean that the offspring of the union were "Lower" than the parents.

God Rested and Lilith Worked

The second chapter of Genesis starts off with a very strange statement. "God Rested". To make it even more bizarre, he rested just as this new man was created and probably needed guidance. Please don't believe the creator God got too tied to do anything and he had to take a nap for a hundred years or something and absolutely don't think the Bible is providing misinformation. It is not. This was Moses' way of telling us that the Nephilim started modifying Homo-Erectus while God simply was seeing how they were doing.

By all accounts, the Nephilim [and the one we will call Lilith] did not rest. They took control of the world. In the Hopi Indian account, some survivors from a terrible war remained and replenished the world. These survivors were the Nephilim and they replenished the Earth by manipulating genetics and some other tricks. The Bible simply indicates God rested. While he was asleep, there was much action.

Genesis 2:1-*Thus the heavens and the Earth were finished, and all the host of them [the heavenly ones] and God ended the work which was made; rested on the seventh day from all his work which he had made.*

God didn't need to sleep, rest, slow down, meditate or anything else. He simply was watching what happened for a time to see how the Nephilim would interact with this 6th day man. Unfortunately, by all accounts, this included sex.

History recorded this as sex between man and Lilith. The Lilith Scientists kept on changing human until Neanderthal was developed about 50 thousand years ago.

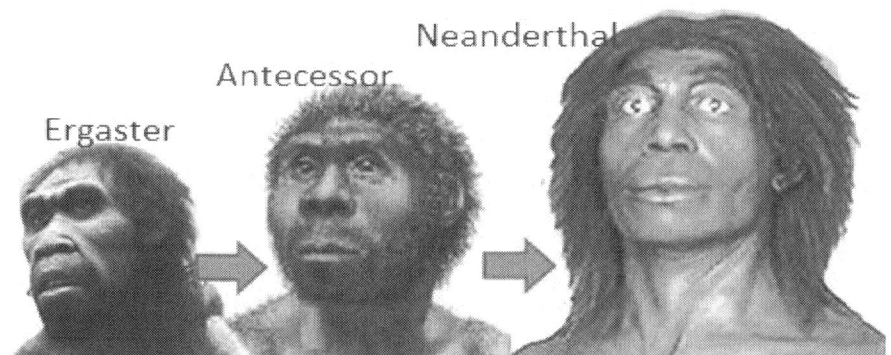

Ready to Mate with Lilith

Neanderthal is about to have Nephilimic/Lilith sex. Not only did the ancient human "Nephilim" help in the changing of animals and man by manipulating genes or some similar action, but after a time, the modified humans had been genetically altered enough so that it was, possibly, now sexually compatible with the Nephilim like Lilith.

The eager Nephilim had offspring with the men and women of Earth and had what the ancient Jewish texts termed as Eljo children [half Nephilim half 6th day-man hybrids]. Some were huge giants with enormous strength. Some were misshapen. You guessed it; the breeder would have been none other than good old Lilith [This was a general term for any of the Nephilim genetic scientists].

Lilith had Some Acceptable Children

Sometimes the offspring were acceptable. The Sumerians have a very detailed description of the change that normally occurred in the "6th day -men" whenever the Nephilim had sex with them. According to the Sumerians, Indians,

Tibetans, Nyombeans, Egyptians, and Aztecs, the same things happened to the primal-human offspring. After inbreeding with the Nephilim, the hair on their body was gone and they no longer were like animals. Let's look at the ancient texts directly and again I must wonder how these things seem to be ignored. We will start with the Jewish account and compare the world accounts.

Jewish Confirmation

The ancient Jewish texts seem to talk about three attempts that were needed to finally make a hybrid man [Eljo]. The scriptures indicate that the sex was not voluntary and, according to the book, "Melchizedek", the men and women talked about at this time were "human", but not the true Adam and Eve. That concept is an important one. According to the ancient accounts, Adam and Eve were not from the same "stock" as all the humans of that day. The Biblical text and many other Jewish texts go to great lengths to establish a difference between the offspring of the Nephilim and human unions and the union of Adam and Eve. They were so emphatic that one would believe that they were trying to make sure we understood the difference.

Too many stories have been written exactly like the ones shown below and they should not be ignored. These stories are all adjuncts to their prospective Adam and Eve stories. This occurrence happened before Adam came along.

Essene Texts

***Enoch 2:18**- Three [Nephilim] came down and copulated with women and had offspring.*

The "three" possibly indicates three successive attempts at inbreeding with humans or three simultaneous inbreeding attempts before the Neanderthal servant was made.

Melchizedek*-Pray for the offspring of the angels, together with seed which flowed forth from the father of all who made the entire universe from nothing there were engendered the gods [Nephilimic humans] and angels, and the men that came out of the seed, all of the natures, those in the heavens and those upon the Earth—now the nature of females was wanting among those that are in the heavens. They were bound with men and women, but these were not the true Adam nor the true Eve.*

This verse talks very clearly about a difference between angels and humans called gods {Nephilim} and infers that a union between man and Nephilim was accomplished. It specifically indicates the human offspring were not the true Adam and Eve. These were probably the Neanderthal servants.

Gnostic Texts

Nag Hammadi "Creation Text"*-Now come let us [the Nephilim] lay hold of her [the human female] and cast our seed into her, so that when she becomes soiled she may not be able to ascend into the light-rather she whom she bares will be under our charge.* This sort of shows why the Nephilim were having sex. They did the sex thing because wanted a servant that would worship them. You guessed it—Neanderthal.

Nag Hammadi [another area]*- [the rulers of the world said] "come let us sow our seed in her [human female]" and they perused her and she laughed at them for their witlessness* *and in their clutches she became a tree and left her shadowy reflection-and they defiled it foully.*

Lilith and the other Nephilim were not always successful at impregnating humans.

Nag Hammadi "Creation Text" again- *[And Samael said] 'come let us create a man out of us; so that when he sees his likeness, he might be enamored by it- We shall make those who are born out of "light" our servants-and their modeled form became an enclosure of the light.- They ignorantly created him-and when they finished Adam, [his soul] abandoned him. Then Lilith] sent her breath into Adam who had no soul. He began to move around.*

Samael was the main instigator. He was the male counterpart to Lilith in Jewish history. Lilith had made the Neanderthal with her breath and possibly other things.

Egyptian Confirmation

This comes from the "Emerald Texts". The details are not stated, but the general picture can be understood.

The master said-take them by the arts ye have learned of far across the waters until ye reach the land of the hairy barbarians [Homo-Erectus], dwelling in caves of the desert. Follow there the plan.

The plan was for "Lilith" to inbreed with the hairy barbarians and continue until they had a reasonable servant [Neanderthal].

Southeast Asian Confirmation

In this ancient story, we find an identical theme. There was a change from Homo-Habilis, to Erectus to Neanderthal all under the watchful control of the Nephilimic humans.

A very hairy human [Homo-Erectus] "female" named Bota Ili was cooking food. [You guessed it; Bota was Lilith.] A "non-hairy" fisherman named Wata Rian saw her and got her drunk. [Sort of a male Lilith character.] While she was asleep, he shaved her entire body [Possibly became Neanderthal]. Only then did he find out she was a woman. She learned to wear clothes, they married, and they began a new race.

Greek Confirmation

The Greek were not as specific, but they did indicate that the early attempts at gods/ Nephilim having offspring with man resulted in monsters.

Greek Mythology-From Greek Mythology we find similar elements. The Nephilim ruled the world and had offspring that were sometimes monstrous. The story of Pandora could have been an attempt at retelling the ancient Lilith story and how she was responsible for many of the ills of the day.

First only existed chaos and Gaia which would be the Earth was formed. Gaia gave birth to the sky. The gods Gaia and Uranos had children-12 were titans, 3 were Cyclopes, and three were monsters with 100 hands. [This is similar to the other texts which indicated that only some of the offspring of Lilith, the Gaia character, were acceptable. Many were monstrous.] *One of the titans took control [Kronos] and created the gods who took control by freeing the monsters. Zeus had a woman created from clay [Pandora]. She opens the box of knowledge and release evil into the world."*

This is the Lilith story. She was made of clay just like Adam, but because the clay was contaminated, she brought forth evil according to the Jewish texts.

The Hopi Story

According to Hopi Historian, Morning Star, in her work "Terra Papers" we learn the following about the Hopi beliefs: It should be noted that, at least part of this work may have been "obtained" from what is called "channeled" information. I have no clue what parts.

The star elders were on earth when the earth was still barren. [Ancient humans were on the earth a long time ago.] *These beings were here throughout evolution* [The ancient humans evolved.] *Sometimes they helped and sometime hurt mankind. Humans were created to be the workers.* [Homo-Erectus were to be workers of the Nephilim] *One of the elders [Lilith] added himself to the humans.* [The Nephilim modified humans by inbreeding.] *The brother of this elder hated what he had done and deposited the "New humans" in the wilderness.* [The new human was no better than the old.] *Later he sent a massive flood to drown them. The original creator god managed to save some of the humans.*

Zoroastrian Beginnings

According to the "ZAND-AKASIH", part of the Zoroastrian Biblical Texts, we find a similar "Neanderthal creation story". Let's see what it had to say. In their story, God was called Ohrmazd. I have changed the name to allow easier reading and after the verses, I have provided comments. The comments are just comments, but please look at similarities of various writings so that you can gain a better perspective of probable truth.

During the fifth time, God created a cow and from it, he created 282 species of animals. He also created Gav [Lilith]; she was white and shining like the Moon. During the 6th time, God created Gayomard. [Modern man was created after his mate.] *Ahriman [Nephilimic humans] miscreated creatures and they became useless. God saw the bad creatures, they did not delight Him. Ahriman's downfall was the unrighteous creation of the creatures.* [Nephilimic Humans like Lilith, modified all the animals.] *Ahriman [the Nephilim] also miscreated Akoman, and the other [Hybrids].* [Akoman was the Neanderthal man.]*Goshorun [Cain], came out of the body of the Gav. God spoke: "Thou art ill, Oh Goshorun; thou hast borne the illness from Ahriman.*

Lilith's Best Creation Neanderthal

That brings us to this special Lilith conversion. If you breed enough " Nephilim into a "normal" human, you will get a substantial change. We find the strange Neanderthal. Nobody has been able to determine where the Neanderthal came from and no one can determine how he finally disappeared. Although he was very similar to the Homo-Erectus, his brain again jumped in size and was now larger than even the brain of today's humans. Many other anomalous features make scientists wonder about this strange human's appearance, but I think there is a logical answer.

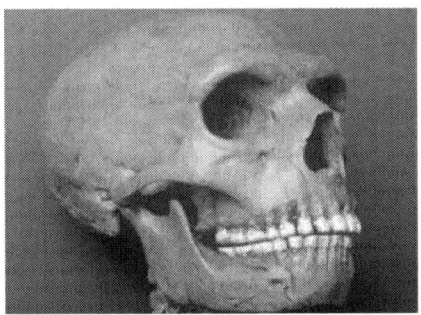 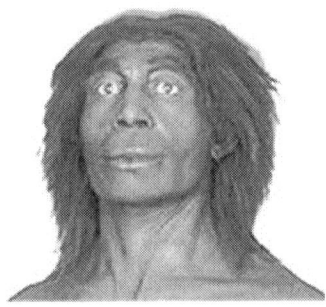

The Neanderthal was, evidently, the hybrid offspring of the union between 6th day man and the Nephilim. If we identify the Nephilim with Lilith, the story continues.

I know the above description sounds like the easy "cop out" answer, but there are many bits of information to lead us to this conclusion.. As shown in the table following, there were marked changes that spontaneously occurred in this "new" human. The changes don't make sense. That is if you don't consider the introduction of "Lilith" crossbreeding.

OK! The big nose doesn't show advancement, but I would imagine that the Neanderthal were proud of their protrusion and ostracized the Homo-Erectus for having the apelike flat nose. The petite nose showed inferiority and they probably wore their large one with pride.

Characteristic NOT found in Erectus	Neanderthal
Alien genes that didn't come from Apes	yes
Brain size greater much than 800 cc	Jumped to 1200cc
Elongated Brain [increased motor skills]	yes
Began to live in villages,	yes
Protected their sick	Yes
Buried their dead	Yes
Worshiped Nephilim and the creator	yes
Began to make jewelry and other non-essential "artworks"	yes
Got shot by a bullet	yes
Red Hair, light complexion	yes
Human Voice	yes
Had Big pronounced Nose	yes

Bullet Head

This Neanderthal was no ancestor to modern man, he was something else. Oh! You are wondering about the bullet comment. You'll have to be the judge. The following graphic left is a picture of a Neanderthal head with a hole from a very high speed tiny projectile. Another is shown to the right. The other side of the skull isn't nearly as pretty. Researchers found more and more holes.

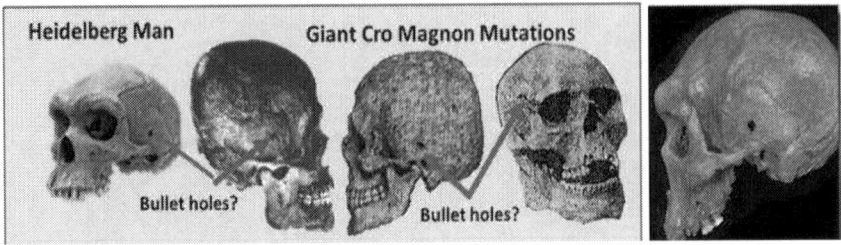

In Russia and extinct Auroch was found with a similar high-speed projectile hole in its forehead which is believed to have been put there during the Pleistocene [See the following collage left]. A similar hole was found in the same type animal in Zambia and other signs of hostilities. Most had a tiny hole going in and much larger exit destruction.

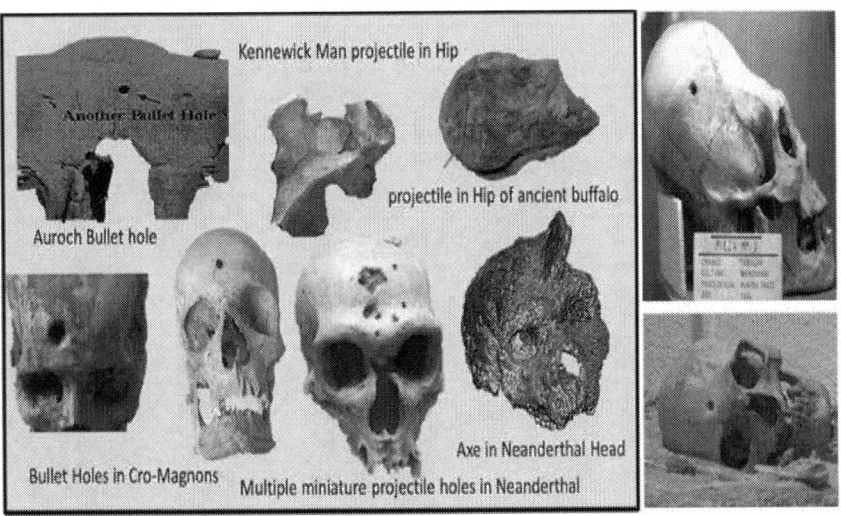

Other skulls have been found with the piculiar holes associated with high speed projectiles and shown next. Some of these may not be from bullets but Neanderthal and Early Cro-Magnon faced more than just animal attacks during the Pleistocene.

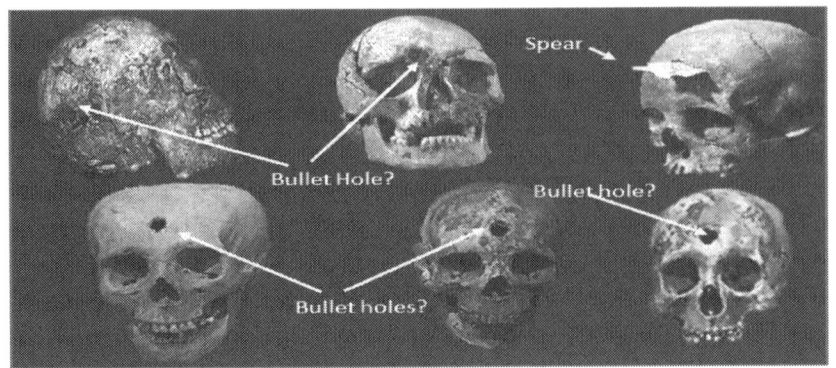

Construction Evidence

With the crude tools, these talented humans built buildings and evidence of their structure can be found today, even after 100 thousand years or more.

Tennessee Wall Making- According to the N.Y. Academy of Sciences, in Bradley County a piece of a wall was uncovered at the surface in 1891. Later it was found to cover a huge area the length of it was traced for 1000 feet. It averaged 8 feet high and 2 feet thick and had projections every 30 feet. It is composed of red sandstone blocks cemented together with a dark red clay mixture. As shown below, it has been recorded that 872 individual hieroglyphic symbols have been found on the blocks. These symbols are assumed some kind of pictographic writing like Chinese.

Spanish Carpentry -According to "Archives of Angryrid", the Viceroy of Peru found a 6 inch long nail inside a boulder in 1572—Iron was unknown to the Peruvian Indians at the time and the nail was estimated to be Tertiary.

Colorado Floor Laying- At a depth of 10 feet in 1936, Tom Kenny found a smooth level pavement made of mortared tiles 5 inches in diameter. Estimated date of the floor was later tertiary.

Kentucky Floor Laying- At Blue Lick Springs was found the remains of a Mastodon some 12 feet below the surface. As excavation continued down to 15 feet, the workers struck a pavement and cut-stone tiles. Most of us know when mastodons became extinct, so how old was the fancy building below?

Arizona Tomb Building- In 1891 an architect named Hendrickson found something eight feet below the foundation line of a hotel. What he found was described as well worked masonry with rose granite blocks and a tomb similar to those found in Egypt. In the tomb was the skeleton of a giant. Over the giant was a grave mask colored blue. The image was of a male with low cheekbones, large nose and mouth. One researcher likened them to the images on Easter Island. He also had six toes and thick bushy hair that reached his shoulders. Battle scenes were engraved on his crown and a large battle-axe accompanied the dead hero. The date was determined by the axe handle. It had been petrified showing the age of the artifact to be Late Tertiary.

Mining Evidence

One of the big things in these early times was mining. Why they mined so much is somewhat of a mystery, and some mines date back substantially before the time of Adam. Not only did these ancients mine workable minerals, but also diamonds mining for diamonds may have simply been picking them up off the ground. Here are a few examples.

Montana Mining- In 1924 the skull of a modern man was found 130 foot deep in a lava covered mine. Estimated age of the lava flow was over 100 thousand years ago.

Nebraska Mining-In 1889 a large 20 pound stone was split open to show a fossil representing a clenched fist of a human, according to the "San Francisco Examiner". The imprint of some type of cloth could be easily seen on the top side of the fossil and when the fossil fist was opened, several small polished diamonds became visible where the cloth may have once been a carrying bag.

Ngwenya African Mining-In Ngwenya, a late Tertiary Hematite mine was found.

Swaziland Mining-An Iron Mine was found in Swaziland, its estimated age was Early Pleistocene.

Shoe Wearing Evidence

The Neanderthal hybrids didn't like standing on hot pavement so they made shoes. Here are some examples.

Nicaragua Shoe Wearing-In 1886, twenty feet down in solid rock footprints and a sandal print were found. The age was estimated to be Later Tertiary and probably was much older. The evenness of the imprint shows these individuals were Homo Sapien Neanderthalis living in the New World before Adam. [See next left]

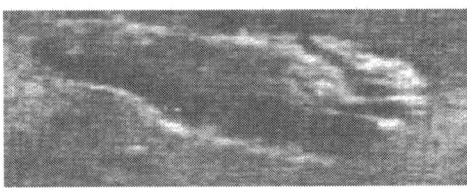

The UK Shoe Wearing-This shoe print [see above right] was found in stone in the U.K.. The person had to be wearing modern shoes and be walking on the ground before the sand had turned to stone; possibly, Tertiary.

Chinese Shoe Wearing-In 1969, according to Dr. Chu Chen, leader of a joint Soviet-Chinese expedition, a perfect imprint of a shoe sole was found embedded in stone. Estimated age was Tertiary.

Manufactured Goods Evidence

The Neanderthal hybrids also manufactured goods. These ancient humans made and used things we normally think of as 20th century goods, evidently without the use of complex tools.

French Tube Making-An Iron Tube was found similar to that shown [below left]. It was estimated to be Later Tertiary.

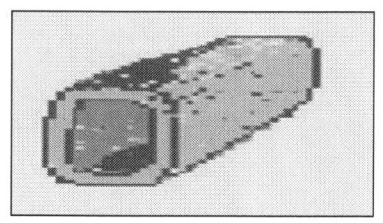 

Massachusetts Vase Making-In 1851, "Scientific American" indicated that a metallic vase was dynamited out of solid Pudding Stone. The vase was 4 ½ inches high and 6 ½ inches at the base and was made of an alloy of zinc and silver. The inside of the vase was inlaid with a floral pattern done in silver. It was found at a depth of 15 feet and its age was estimated to be Later Tertiary. The graphic to the right in the previous graphic shows a reconstruction of vase. All but the handle was found.

Illinois Coinage-I 1870, in a 100 foot deep hole, a coin or quarter sized medallion, made of copper alloy, was found. The coin had an etching of a woman and a form of what appeared to be alphabetic letters. Estimated age of the coin was again, Later Tertiary. The drawing below shows what it looked like.

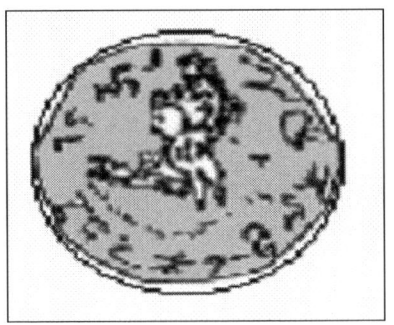 

Costa Rican Sphere Making-Spheres have been found everywhere. Some scientists believe that the giant stone spheres were made in the very ancient times, but no one knows when. Some spheres are over two meters in diameter, and yet are almost perfectly spherical. They are made from a wide assortment of materials including granite, andesite, and even sedimentary stone, and weigh up to 16 tons. One theory is that they were placed around to represent a gigantic star pattern. One is shown above.

Toys & Jewelry Evidence

These creative humans were not just surviving, but there complex society included the manufacture and use of dolls as playthings.

Ljubljanaian Flute Making- What has been termed the Neanderthal flute segment, estimated at about up to 80 thousand years old, was found recently by Dr. Ivan Turk, a paleontologist at the Slovenian Academy of Sciences in Ljubljana. [See below]

Idahoan Toy Making-In 1912, a clay figurine was found. The figurine was of a woman and was 2 ½ inches long. It was found while digging down to a depth of 300 feet. Its estimated age was Tertiary. One of the legs was not found and was added in the image above, to show what the full figure doll looked like when the hybrids made it.

Neanderthal Shell Art-A shell was found with an intricate depiction of a face. The estimated age of the time when the shell was dropped was later Tertiary.

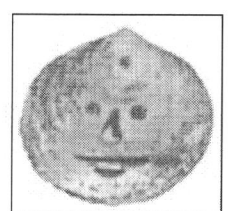 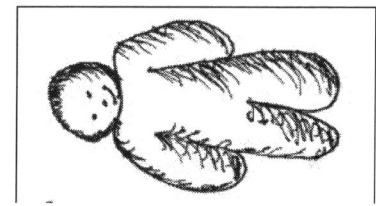

Ohioan Doll Making- In 1880, another doll figure was found at a depth of 120 feet while drilling a well, but this one was found in Ohio. It was made in black variegated marble and was 6 inches tall. It had very similar characteristics to the one found in Idaho.

Californian Stone Carving- In 1964 an 800-pound, intricately carved, stone was found. Its estimated age was pre-Ice Age; possibly, Tertiary.

Neanderthal Jewelry Making-Several sites have provided elements that were jewelry items. Jewelry is typical of civilized people. Note the necklace beads found. Even today, we use cowry shells for necklaces. The string is not part of the find.

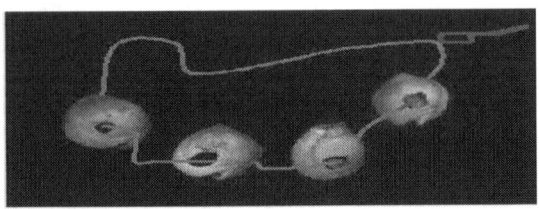

Lilith's Alien Gene

Before we can understand Neanderthal, we must first accept one thing. The "Homo-Erectus" base was continuously manipulated genetically to characterize the perfect worker for the Nephilim and the Neanderthal was the ultimate achievement. Over the last 150 years, scientists have struggled to unravel the mystery of the Neanderthals without the acceptance of this important piece of the puzzle. Of course, their conclusions are very limited because they tried to separate science and religion. The first significant discovery was made in August 1856. A partial skeleton was found at the Feldhofer Cave in the Neander Valley, in Germany. This was the find that gave the species its name. Since then over 500 individuals have been found from over 80 sites in Europe, the Middle East and parts of Western Asia along with several hundred thousand stone tools.

Neanderthal the Alien

It wasn't until 1997 that a small scrap of DNA was discovered which showed "Alien Genetics" with respect to our own DNA or that of an ape. Neanderthal could not have come from either group "exclusively" as neither group contained portions of the DNA found in Neanderthal. This further confused the already misaligned groups of

Paleoanthropologists. Besides the physical elements and no common ancestor, here are some of the things we have been told about the Neanderthal species as a social animal.

- *Some of them were cannibalistic as determined from a Moula-Guercy, France site evidence.*
- *There was hybridization between Cro-Magnon and Neanderthal about 25 thousand years ago as evidenced from a recent Portuguese find showing many ambiguous characteristics.*
- *Even though the Neanderthal, as a species, lived for many thousands of years, they continued to use rudimentary tools and weapons. [This anomaly is very puzzling given the fact that Neanderthal had a larger brain than modern man, but there may be a good reason for this strange fact. A theory of this anomaly will be presented later.]*
- *The majority of the "pure Neanderthal" stayed in the European area.*
- *They began the custom of elongating their heads artificially, showing a strong reverence to some type of long headed humans. [Later we will also see the significance of this strange custom, so don't forget this element while we look at his brain.]*

Neanderthal Brain Expansion

While we are on the subject of Neanderthal heads, we need to discuss brains, because, like I said before, Neanderthal had a larger brain and the brain was shaped substantially different than the "Modern Man Brain". The Neanderthal brain was much longer as shown next by the elongated skull on the right as compared to the modern skull on the extreme left.

This enlarged brain was not due to evolution, because its change is drastic. It came from Lilith's inbreeding.

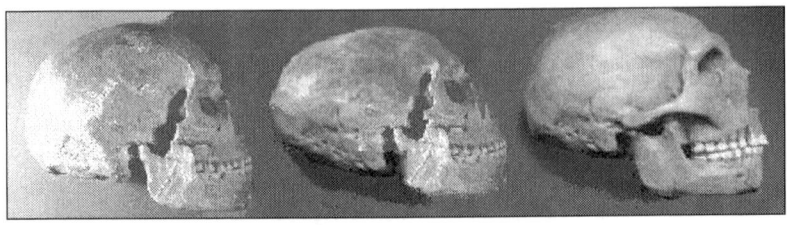

Modern   European   Neanderthal

The chart following shows the general progression of brain size to humanoid type and mean period of existence. The vertical lines represent the range of brain sizes determined for each of the subgroups. Note the sharp slope as brain sizes began expanding faster and faster until the Neanderthal. The brain atrophy thing appears to have something to do with the UFO's that have been seen in recent years, so it will not be covered here.

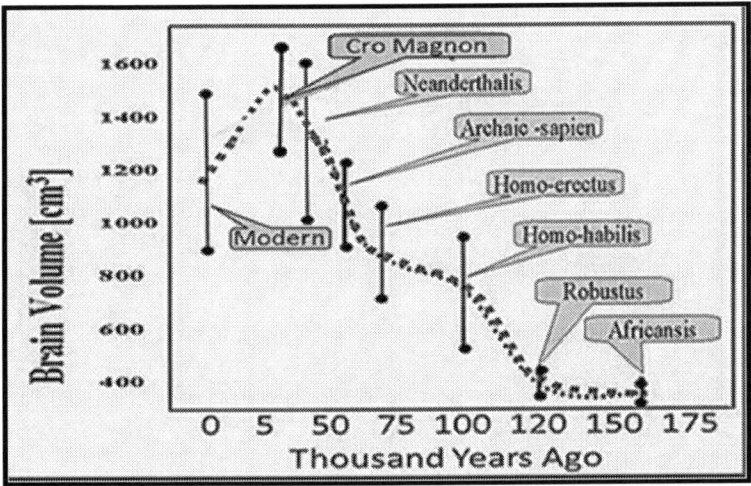

By the way, this chart does not include the anomalous Dolichocephalic/Homo Capensis giants associated with Lilith. While the skinny headed giants were rulers of the world after the world-wide flood. Their development was caused by them rather than them having a similar "evolution".

European Neanderthal

To make things even more interesting, the brain shape of ancient European "Homo Sapien-Sapiens", as shown by the middle skull image are more closely identified with the Neanderthal than those of the Middle Eastern Homo-Sapien-Sapien [left] brains. This whole" long flat brain" and the "round brain" anomaly should be investigated further, because Neanderthal didn't make complex tools and his flat brain may tell us why. I'm going to wait a little before I finish the comments about European brains, but remember it while we continue.

Neanderthal Brain Anomaly

The huge brain of this species means that Neanderthal was a smart individual. In some respects, he was smarter than today's humans who suffer from brain atrophy. Our shrinking brain isn't going to be covered in this book, but it is very interesting just the same.

Some will argue that having a large brain does not necessarily mean the individual is smart. That comment seems to be a crazy assertion, usually made by someone with a small brain.

It's like saying that the dinosaurs were smart because they had tiny brains. Even more than being smart, the difference in shape suggests something else. He had capabilities we do not have nor possibly ever had in our ancient past. I don't know what those were, but the large back portion of the Neanderthal brain suggests that they had to do with enhanced sight, hearing, and motor skills. That's right I said motor skills. He wasn't a lumbering individual and must have been able to perform maneuvers we cannot begin to achieve today with respect to hand-eye coordinated efforts. He had been engineered to be a fantastic worker for the Nephilim.

Neanderthal Articulation

According to a large amount of physical evidence, the Lilith bred Neanderthal could punch very clean holes through bones for talismans and they did this remarkable feat with very rudimentary tools. This by itself does not show enhanced articulation, but it is a clue. We may also notice that European craftsmanship is highly praised today and the European brains, at least the early ones, seem to be in between Neanderthal and the other "modern" human brains. Perhaps we should infer that a large back portion of the brain denotes enhanced articulation.

Neanderthal Creativity

The other thing that is noticeable is the fact that the "central creativity lobe" is smaller which makes the brain more flattened than our current brains. This suggests that their creativity level was not up to our potential. Whenever the new creation was established, some of these features were not necessary and therefore were not integrated into the design of the man/hybrid. With less creativity came less advancement. Neanderthal made and used only very rudimentary tools even though he was very smart. The two don't seem to go together, but what we will find out is that this hybrid man may not have needed any special tools and his creativity level did not make him investigate newer ways to do things once an adequate method had been reached. Lack of curiosity evidently killed this cat [I mean Neanderthal].

Neanderthal Made a Good Servant

These very articulate, highly intelligent, extremely strong workers would have taken more time to develop his society with this lower level of creativity, but that did not mean that he wasn't very good at what he was made for. He was made [by Lilith] to be a worker. He worked in huge mining fields that have been found around the world. He worked in the fields; he worked on construction sites; and he worked for the master race of Nephilim until "the new Adam" was created. Then, according to Biblical texts and other documents, within one generation we find that humans changed overnight. They became creative and curious. We find the following:

- *Substantial metalworking,*
- *Manufacturing of war materials [the bullet holes in the Neanderthal human did not come from another Neanderthal]*
- *Use of colors in his artwork*
- *Great expansion of music*
- *Manufacturing of very complex tools*

As each new discovery was made by the Adamic human, I can hear the Neanderthal saying---"Why didn't I think of that?" The reason was the shape of his brain.

Destined for Extinction

Besides his large, intelligent but uncreative brain, the Neanderthal was a true offshoot with no place to go, [or so it would seem]. Let's look at man's progression pictorially. If we take the basic progression of man normally identified and modify it slightly, then the Neanderthal, being a combination of Erectus and the Nephilimic breeders may be more important. The "modern man" indicated in this diagram is not necessarily from Adam, but the Neanderthal certainly is not related in any substantial way until he may have bred with the descendants of Cain in the land of Nod.

Tails-You may note the tails in the diagrams. The tail bone of modern humans is much more pointed than that of the Neanderthal. One reason might be that miniature tails were evident on the earlier humanoids, but that is also a different story.

Europe and the Aryan Race

Possibility of tails is one thing, but I know I'm getting into trouble here. The question is, "What does the European and Neanderthal similarity mean with respect to heritage?" Aren't Europeans the remains of the Aryan Race and didn't their ancestors come from Adam?? ---The answer is they are not Aryan and they are not completely Adamic.

Not only are the Europeans not the Aryan race, they are not something else. They are not from Cro Magnon or at least they are not exclusively from the race started by Adam and Eve. Here is some more bad news for those shocked by this statement. The Bible and other ancient texts confirm it. While this subject is way to touchy for this book, let me just say that if your ancestors did not have a round head, you must have come from a different group that those who began with round heads. The other thing that should be remembered is that there has been so much intermarriage that it doesn't matter much today anyway. Everyone today are mixed Gentile humans. There are no pure Jewish Cro-Magnon and none of the Homo Erectus or Neanderthal made it past the Pleistocene Extinction. Instead some with Neanderthal blood made it as a hybrid from the Pleistocene mixed with the bloodline of Cain and the Nephilim.

Neanderthal in America

Everyone indicates that no Lilith bred Neanderthal have been found in the new world, but let's look at the Maya. Their facial characteristics were very similar to the Neanderthal and they were fairly short and heavy built like the Neanderthal. In DNA studies, South America has about the highest similarity to Neanderthal. This is much higher than the level seen in Europeans where almost all the Neanderthal skeletons were found.

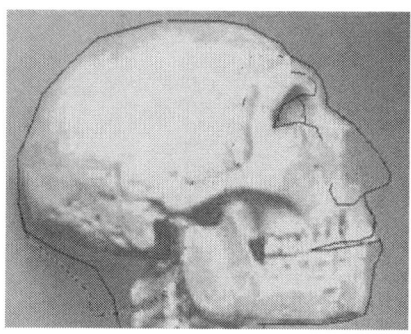

As shown above, the Neanderthal had a huge nose, receding chin, large brow ridges, low sloping forehead and the middle of his face was pulled forward while the cheek bones sloped backwards. The rest of his body was ruggedly built. These distinctive characteristics would make him easy to spot in a crowd today, and the Maya even looked similar as shown above right.

Neanderthal Got Too Smart

Whenever Lilith or whoever mated with the Homo-Erectus humans, the offspring began to get very smart. From the evidence of the fossils, it took many tries before man was as smart as a Nephilim and, unfortunately for him, most of his teaching was from Nephilim rather than from God. These offspring soon could reason to a high level and were taught "flying, war, weapons of war, and many other things for which they were not ready. <u>The Nephilim wanted servants, but according to the Nag Hammadi texts and other texts, man was too smart to serve the Nephilim.</u>

This is when God again steps back into the picture. The Bible indicates he woke up and began to recreate a new human. He called this new human, Adam. In order to try to keep this new human from learning too much of the ways of the Nephilimic humans, he warned the new human to stay away from the tree of knowledge. Whether this is a real thing or a symbolic direction to stay away from Nephilim that would not keep the new humans "pure" is not determined in this book, but there is strong evidence that there was a continuous fight between the two major human groups of the day the Nephilim [along with their servants] and the new Adamic human. This portion of our story may seem in more violation with basic beliefs than the first portion simply because we talk about this portion more. Let's get everyone concerned right away by saying that Adam's first wife was named Lilith. She was different than him. One thing that shows she was different is that she may have been the father of Cain.

Lilith #2- Nephilimic Wife to Adam, consort to Samael, Reptilian shapeshifter, and "Father" to Cain

Lilith, Adam's 1st Wife

Lilith as the initiator of humanity before the time of Adam is one thing, but now I'm going to violate the very essence of what we thought we knew about the Biblical time of Adam. What I'm talking about is that a "human" named Lilith was, according to many ancient texts, the 1st wife of Adam.

The stories are numerous and are told both by the ancient Jewish people and others around the world. So without further ado, here goes our second phase- *the story of Lilith, Adam's first wife.* Some of these references to "Adam" may be talking about the 6th day man rather than the creation that we typically call Adam. You'll have to bear with this level of confusion as several of the stories of ancient women all call the name of the female "Lilith". The texts also call several different human creations "Adam". I put together a chart to show how the Adamics, People of Cain, the Nephilim and the Neanderthal type humans comingled according to anceint texts.

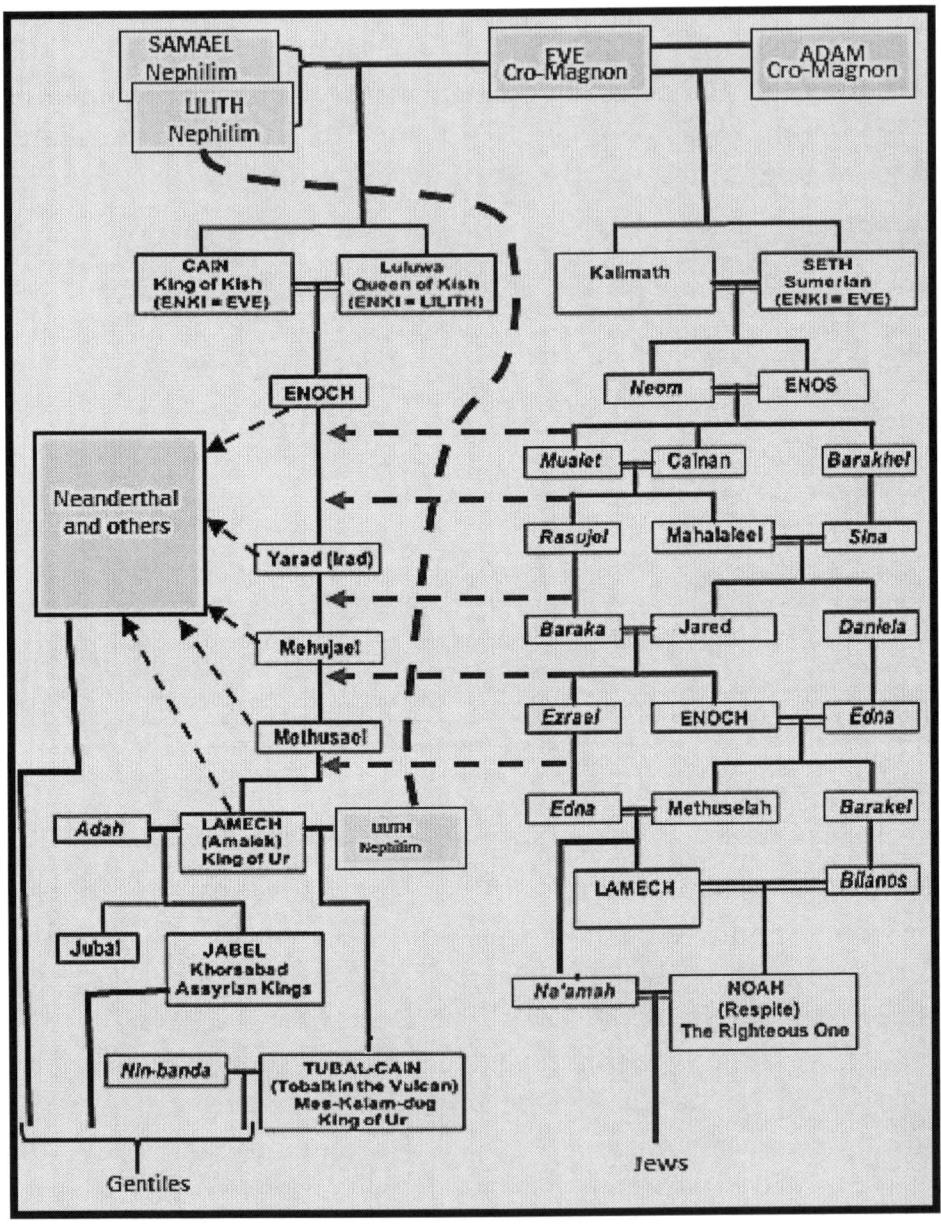

This next graphic shows the Lilith#1 as Homo-Capensis/ Nephilim and she made the 8 or so variation of God's Homo-Erectus during the Tertiary period. It also shows the Anak, Cro Magnon and the 10 major types of Gentiles scientists have determined by DNA mutations and possibly Lilith intervention during the Pleistocene. The last column show the 29 major races by major mutational difference. That has little to do with Lilith, but it was already on the chart.

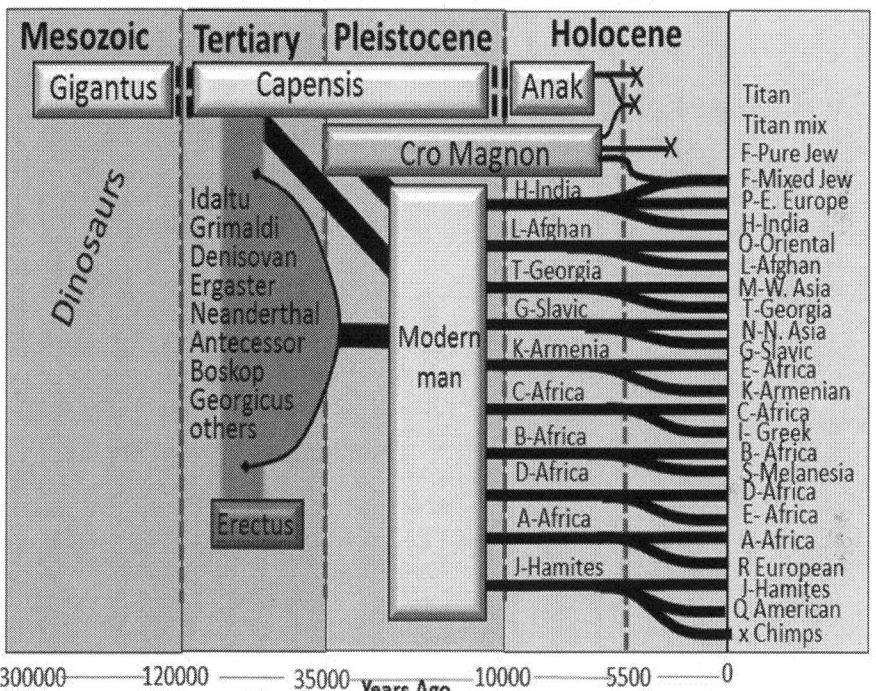

Possibly Not Adam's Wife

Don't just take for granted that Lilith was Adam's first wife as indicated in early writings, but don't ignore the stories either. The preceding figure shows one of the depictions of Lilith over the years. She is the one in the tree in the first image. Temptress and wily "serpent", she has been revered and feared for many, many years. The reasons behind the serpent will be evident as we discuss the Garden of Eden and what she [or another Lilith] did to disrupt paradise. Right now, let's try to understand the basic stories.

Lilith the Dirt Woman

The Lilith Story was probably started to explain evolution. As soon as God made man, we are told in ancient Jewish literature, that there was a woman, made of impure sediments that became Adam's first wife. We can believe the reference was to show she was one of the impure Nephilim women. They go on to say she was evil and sister to Samael and the two became the Conjurer/Serpent identified in Genesis. Many stories about Lilith were written in ancient days and retold by the early Jewish people concerning this event. The story is probably in reference to the female Nephilim that actually had sex with the ape-men and created the hybrid men.

While reading the various Lilith stories, think back to the Greek myths you learned in high school and remember how the "gods" kept on having sex with mortals. Sometimes the offspring were monsters and sometimes they were saints. Remember that <u>Zeus had sex with over 100 women</u> and he was the head Nephilim or Olympian gods. Some of those stories were probably telling a very close proximity to the truth, but they were presented in our schools as fiction so most of us took them to be fictitious. Now we find out that when many ancient stories are melded together, they form a picture not far away from the basic Geek myths we laughed at.

Lilith Hybrids Died at Birth

Ancient histories tell us Lilith got pregnant often, the babies usually died. This portion of the Lilith story seems to indicate that most of the offspring from the union of Nephilim and these early men did not survive, but later we will see that offspring from these types of unions and a new creation of mankind were more successful. That is not to say that the offspring always survived, but many of the offspring that did survive were considered to be gentiles. Later hybrids became more Nephilimic and were considered to be demigods. This concept is an important one as we study our history. If it is hard to believe that these ancient humans were having sex with less ancient humans and that the outcome of the union caused offspring to be born which had special capabilities, I feel the same way. Unfortunately, evidence will be presented in this book to confirm the stories.

Lilith & the Bible

The Bible was not left out in the whole Lilith world. Ancient Biblical and Dead Sea scroll information about Lilith is limited, but evidence is provided that the ancients knew about the Lilith story and believed the essence of it. Later the details of Naamah, as a daughter of Lilith, and stories about how she fits into the picture will strengthen the Lilith Stories and the Biblical connection even further.

Isaiah 34:14-The wild beasts of the desert shall also meet with the wild beasts of the island, and the satyr [genetic mutation] shall cry to his fellow; <u>Lilith also shall rest there</u>, and find for herself a place of rest. [This is the only remaining reference in the <u>current</u> Old Testament to Lilith besides the wife of Lamech descriptions.]

Songs of the Sage-all the spirits of the ravaging angels and the bastard spirits, demons<u>, Liliths, and those who strike unexpectedly to lead astray the spirit of knowledge</u> [the Nephilim taught man the wrong kind of knowledge].

Genesis 4:20:22-*Lamech took unto him two wives: the name of the one was Adah, and the name of the other Zillah [Lilith]. And Zillah, she also bare Tubal-Cain, an instructor of every artificer in brass and iron: and the sister of Tubal Cain was Naamah [Remember her name when we talk about the Zohar. She was not only her daughter, but also her accomplice].*

Lilith Adam's First Wife from the Cabala

Yalqut 34b-*The holy one created woman, and she was not flesh but impure sediment-she was a harmful spirit [Nephilim]-the Holy One took her away from Adam and gave him another [Eve].*

Alphabet *of* Ben Sira-*The gods created [man] Adam who was alone-then he created woman for Adam from the Earth and called her Lilith-they began to fight [because Adam wanted to dominate her] and Lilith left.*

Zohar 3:19-*There was a female, her name was Lilith, and she was first with Adam [man]-- God formed Lilith, the first woman, except he used sediment instead of pure dust.-When Lilith saw Adam attached to Eve, she fled and later tried to harm the sons of man.*

Lilith & Casey

The twentieth century seer, Edger Cayce provides us with a picture of Lilith that is similar to the ancient works, but puts blame of monstrous creatures being created directly on modern man for misuse of his free-will and the eventual development of the monstrous creatures. We will see later that the monsters and giants try to take over.

Edger Cayce-*The first female was Lilith, Eve's forerunner. From her many monstrosities came to be- centaurs, satyrs,* *unicorns, and other forms known to us through myth. Realize that these creations were not God's, but rather OUR own that came about because of our own misuse of free will".*

Incan Lilith

According to the Inca, this hybrid man had too much knowledge and no memory of God. The hybrids would not worship the angels. This smartness was the beginning of the Lilith Story. Mankind would not subserviate himself to the Nephilim "Lilith" and the Nephilim got angry.

Popul Vuh- *"Then the gods made humans a second time out of wood [by genetic manipulation]--. Let us make him who will nourish and sustain us. We have tried with our first creations, our first creatures; but we could not make them praise and venerate us.*

So, then, let us try to make obedient, respectful beings. The creations looked like real people, but did not praise god because they had no memory, had no souls, and learned too much. Finally, they made creatures to which spiritual beings could attach. [Yes, that's right, they had sex with the creations they had just made.]

The Nephilim, like Lilith, taught this hybrid-man too much about the worldly things then modified them so that they could reproduce with the Nephilim. Lilith wasn't called out by name, but the sex was the same as other stories that follow.

Three Faces of Lilith

While it is difficult to separate the three entities of Lilith, the general depictions shown next generally show the main difference- Nephilim, Snake woman, and Demoness.

The first is the Sumerian Goddess who was friend of the Owls; the second is the "part serpent part female" seductress of the Garden of Eden; and the last is the evil demoness that would come for children and the souls of men. The seductress part didn't stay in the past as the writers of the Jewish "Cabbala" warn everyone to try to escape the wandering of the "spirit of Lilith", but that part of our story will have to wait. We are only now coming to the second emanation.

Lilith Turning to A "Reptilian-Conjurer"

Descriptions of Lilith

The second Lilith has a simple story. She originally married Adam, but Adam wanted to be the ruler of the family and text say Lilith got mad and FLEW away. When she came back, Adam was with Eve and she got together with another Nephilim "Samael" and together they became serpent-like. As this very handsome reptilian-man, seduced and had relations with Eve so she ate from the tree of knowledge to bring sin to the world. Adam did the same,

This made God angry and he cursed Lilith such that she and her descendants would have the following punishments.

1. *She and the other Nephilim associated with her would never leave the Earth, even after death. [**Genesis 3:14**- You will crawl on your belly and eat the dust of the earth forever.]*
2. *She would be detestable to Humans in appearance—even reptilian. [**Genesis 3:15** Adam's people will become enemies and crush your head.]*
3. *She could never have children by the Cro-Magnon again, but later we find she could have children by Cain's children, so this was a minor setback. [**Genesis 3:15**- There will be enmity between your seed and Adam's seed.]*

Researchers would find that a large number of serpent-like people were integrated into societies of Gentile populations so it appears while they lived, the descendants of Lilith after the punishment had to stay reptilian-like until they all died off about 6 thousand years ago. The Cabala made no bones about it. Let's read the Zohar.

Zohar 1:147b*-Adam was seduced by her, he sinned with that whore of a woman, the primordial serpent ---*

To get a better felling about this secondary description of this strange person, let's look at some of the countless depictions of Lilith through the years. She is typically associated with owls and reptiles along with the seduction of men. She was generally considered a god by the people of the time. Sometimes she was a snake. Below are some of the depictions of this powerful ancient woman.

Lilith and the Egyptians

The Egyptians called Lilith "Isis", but I think you will quickly see that they are one and the same. The following is from the Egyptian "Legend of Ra and Isis".

Isis/Lilith*-Behold the goddess Isis lived in the form of a woman who had the knowledge of words. [Just like Lilith, Isis is sometimes a woman and sometimes a Nephilim.]Her heart turned away in disgust from the millions of men and she chose for herself the millions of gods, but esteemed more highly the millions of spirits.*

This tells us that gods/Nephilim were less than the spirits/angels.

Was it not possible to become even as was Ra in heaven and upon earth, and make herself mistress of the earth. [Just like the Biblical version, Lilith or the Nephilim wanted to gain back the heaven-key that they had lost in the Heaven war.]Ra entered heaven and established himself on the double throne. Now he had become old and dribbled at the mouth and his spittle fell upon the earth.

If we assume that the Ra figure is none other than the Nephilim named Satan, it makes since that he would be getting old after he no longer ate fruit from the tree of life .

Isis kneaded it in her hand with some dust and <u>she fashioned it in the form of a serpent</u>.

Just like the Lilith stories, Isis was able to make or become a serpent.

Lilith & the Middle East

***Jewish-Lilith**—she was an evil temptress, heartless. She would generally visit men in their sleep, have sex and give birth to demons. When joined with Samael would become a serpent that could seduce women.* [This probably means that male Nephilim had sex with ape-women and produced hybrids.]

Chinese Lilith - Nu Gua

This account comes from Chinese mythology including, "Huai Nan Zi", written about 200 BC, and "Story of Pan Gu" from about the 3rd century AD, but I'm sure you will see many of the same elements as depicted by everyone else.

Then Pan Gu made humans out of mud. [These people were made before the age of man and are re-created later.] *Pan Gu died and the first ruler of the world reigned for 18 thousand years.*

<u>He took the form of a great serpent</u> with 12 heads and animal legs. Then his son took control and reigned for 18 thousand years. <u>He also looked like a serpent</u>. After that came the 10

epochs of man [Notice the 36 thousand years is similar to the time period of book three.]

The land of Huaxu was an earthly paradise. Men lived to a very great age there by eating a special peach. [The Garden of Eden is the same except that the fruit of immortality was a peach.]

While walking one day, one of the maidens stepped on the indention left by a giant's foot. [Just like the offspring of the Nephadim, Giants lived at this time.]

She got pregnant because of this and Fu Xi was born [Humans and non-humans have children together.]

Nu Wa was wife to Fu Xi. When Nu Wa and FuXi were joined together, <u>they became like serpents</u> with tails instead of legs . [Very similar to the Lilith story.]

Nu Wa also molded man out of mud. [Man is recreated.]

It is identical to the Jewish story of Samael and Lilith getting together to form a serpent. The drawing to the left shows Nu Gua. If you didn't know it, you would think she was Lilith. The second drawing is also of the Chinese version of Lilith. Except for the odd Chinese hat, it is identical to the other depictions of Lilith.

Lilith in Europe

In Europe, the names changed, but the characteristics stayed the same. There were actually two distinct personalities. She was the spirit seducer of men, and demon maker; and she part human part serpent often associated with the Garden of Eden..

Lilith with Wings-In this German wood carving, Lilith is seen with wings. The Cabbala agrees with this depiction in that Lilith flew away when she got angry with Adam.

Other Depictions of the medieval times include those shown before with transitions from serpent loving female to the serpent itself.

Lilith in India

Certainly, this goddess to the spirit of the tree of life is referencing the same Lilith stories. Especially as we consider the Lilith stories quickly expanded to become part of the Serpent in the Garden of Eden.

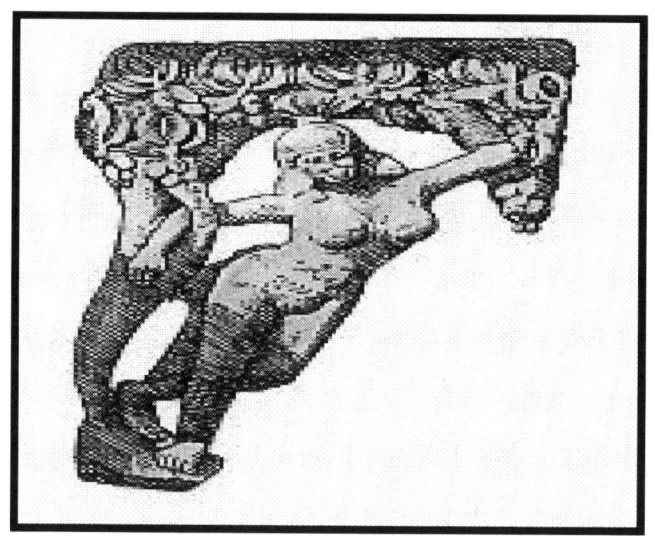

We are now getting into the second depiction. We are coming to the time of Adam and Eve. In this Lilith story, she is the first wife of Adam and she has some amazing tricks. Our initial descriptions come from the Cabbala.

Pictures of Lilith

Somehow the idea of a handsome conjurer turned into a snake in the Garden and many painters changes Lilith images forever. Below are some of the hundreds of depictions of Lilith. Notice that she is usually depicted as part human and part snake or reptile just like the depictions of Seraphim. Lilith could very well have been a Nephilimic version of a Seraphimic Angel that was able to finally mate with the humans. In the Cabala, Lilith is depicted as the seducer of both Adam and Eve.

Lilith was many times depicted as a snake lover. This probably stems from the fact that many Lilith stories involve her turning into a snake or having serpent qualities.

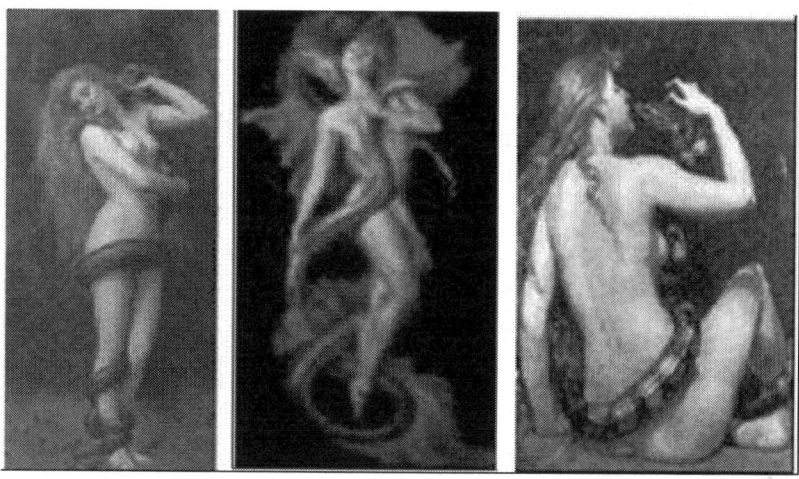

She begins her transformation. First, a tail begins to emerge as shown below. Her true nature is described and her capability of turning into a reptile is apparent. Sometimes wings appear, but usually the only apparent change is reptilian.

Her legs go away, but her arms stay in place as shown below.

Her arms turn into snake-like appendages. Completely useless but still in place.

Soon, only the head of a woman is apparent. The rest of the body is completely snakelike.

Finally, she has completely changed into a snake.

The most memorable image of Lilith has been reproduced repeatedly. Some of you probably have seen some of these depictions, but simply decided that the serpent in the garden was a female. You also probably thought that this female seduced Eve, even if that doesn't make much sense.

The following left is the Michael Angelo version from the Vatican. He liked the one with arms.

While these all seem strange, their strangeness is amplified as we see similar depictions around the world. The thing that is common is an underlying element of inappropriate sex between the Nephilim and the other humans.

Zohar 1:148a-*The male is called Samael, his female [Lilith] is always included within him. Male and female embracing one another.* <u>*The female of Samael is called Serpent.*</u>

Zohar 1:19-*Samael resembles the form of Adam, -and Lilith [Lilith#2] the form of Eve.* <u>*Together, the serpent.*</u>

To make it even more remarkable is the fact that Adam probably had difficulty having sex or having children. Before we go on, I apologize for this section.

Difficulty With Sex

Many now maintain that "Adamic Man", originally, was neither designed nor engineered to procreate so Lilith had a hard time with the new Cro-Magnon man. The Bible supports this theory as we were told that, *"Adam could not find a helpmeet"* after he was initially created. This curious verse seemed to indicate that procreation with a female was difficult.

No Penis Bone

It is even more curious when one knows that a human male is almost the only mammal that does not have a penis, bone or Baculum, to allow for reasonable and quick intercourse. A small sample is shown below along with the Walrus Baculum that can be 22 inches long.

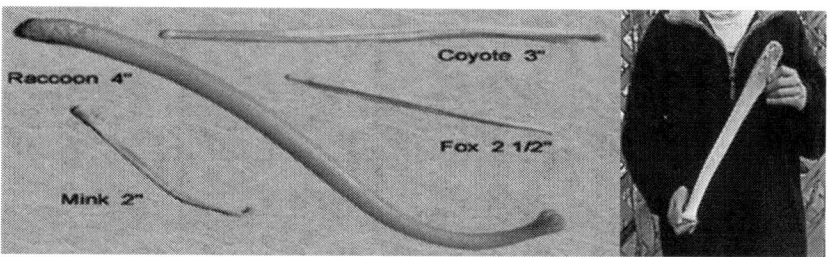

This new human was not initially made for procreation so a woman was not made for him at first. I'm not getting into the details of this odd characteristic, but God saw that Adam was miserable and finally made Eve from Adam's own body so that procreation would be possible. Even offspring of Adam may have been lacking in the procreative capability. We find in the Zohar this interesting verse.

***Zohar 1:19b**-When Cain was born, Lilith could not attach herself with him—[This attachment was sexual attachment.]*

The Homo-Erectus, on the other hand was created to REplenish the Earth, so we can believe that group of humans. This group mated with the descendants of Cain and, finally, we read that Lilith had 2 children by Lamech, Cain's great grandson reversing Lilith's initial problem. Anyway; this new Adamic human had a more difficult time with procreation and Lilith might have seen a new opportunity to get in good with Adam.

Lilith Came Back

Originally, Adam's first wife, who we call Lilith supposedly left the company of Adam over a power struggle.

With Eve having trouble in childbirth, she came back. According to several ancient accounts, Lilith originally did not want to subserviate herself to man and left Adam. Some stories suggest that this "woman that jilted Adam" was not made on the 8th day, but instead, was a Nephilim as we have brought out at the beginning of this book. Naturally, she would not be only his wife as Adam required if she was a Nephilim. Whether she was made with Adam or was a Nephilim didn't matter because she left Adam and he could no longer find a helpmeet, according to the book of Genesis.

Lilith did not go completely away. When Adam got his new "rib woman" [Eve], ancient texts indicate she plotted with Samael [the serpent] to bring Adam and Eve down from their close union with God. We are told by the ancient writings that Lilith and Samael became as one and together they were in the form of a serpent. In this "reptilian" form, they seduced Eve together. The union was successful and, from the union, Cain was born. I know I stepped in it again, but this possibility is confirmed by several ancient texts.

Lilith in the Garden

As I brought out; in the Garden of Eden when Lilith was combined with Samael, she became the serpent that tempted Eve. The Zohar described the seduction very crudely.

Who was Lilith Again?-I'm sure some of you are fuming by now, but remember that these are alternatives that need to be considered, and they are not the only answer that makes up the truth, so bear with me. As you probably have guessed by now Lilith is a hard entity to define. Possibly, she was the Nephilimic mother of the 6th day man, but another Lilith may also have been Adam's first wife. As his first wife, she is described as the mother of Cain, but both Eve and Lilith may both have been the mother.. If she was his mother or if she was, indeed a Nephilim, there were reasons to fear the doom that was brought about by her inbreeding.

The writings concerning Lilith represent more than one being, and that's exactly what makes them so difficult to interpret. Below are definitions of three separate Lilith entities. Each time you read about her, you need to consider which one of the following, the text may be talking about.

Nephilimic Lilith-The original Lilith probably represented a Nephilim that bred with the sixth day man. As a Nephilim, the very mystic descriptions and those which discuss some awesome power of Lilith would be referring to her. Because of a curse placed on interaction between the Nephilim/serpent and Eve, the Nephilim and Adamics could not have children together after Adam and Eve ate the "forbidden fruit". Before the curse, this version of Lilith was extremely beautiful and after the curse, she became ugly and reptilian. Ancient Jewish texts talk about how ugly the Seraphimic Nephilim were, so they may have been talking about the descendants of Lilith. You also may be thinking that this curse is what caused the seraphim to become ugly just like I do. Let's see what the Jewish historians had to say in three different books.

"Origins of the World"-He created other, serpent-like angels, called "Seraphim", which praise him at all times. [In this ancient writing, there is no mistake that the seraphim looked like a reptile.]

"Isaiah 6:2"- Above it stood the seraphim: each one had six wings; with twain he covered his face [now you know why

he covered his face], *and with twain he covered his feet, and with twain he did fly.*

"Testament of Amram"- *One of them [Two beings were fighting over Amram] was terrifying, like a serpent. He was many-colored and dark. His visage was like a viper and wearing __, and all of his eyes __.* [Multiple eyes, terrifying serpent features; Amram must have seen seraphim.]

Adamic-like Lilith-Many documents indicate that Lilith was one of the wives of Adam. From most accounts, this Lilith was not reverent to God or Adam. Because she would have been an Adamic human, and she could certainly mate with Adamics without problem. Her offspring probably would have been those residents in the land of Nod that were living there when Cain was exiled. She probably had many children before the curse that was placed on Eve and the serpent, or should I say Adamics and Nephilim. The cures was then a controlling factor as it made human offspring from a Nephilim and Adamic union an almost impossibility. This means that that there were, probably, many hybrids that were half Adamic and half Nephilimic.

Hybrid Lilith-The mother of Tubal-Cain and Naamah was also sometimes known as Lilith. If this was another Lilith, she was, most likely, a hybrid that was part Nephilim part Adamic human. In some instances, she was known as Zillah. She strengthened the union between Cain's offspring and the Nephilim. This is only mentioned for completeness as this Lilith had little to do with our history.

With all the machinations, no wonder people get confused about Adam's wives.

Lilith Hands Out Fruit

Many texts discuss the Nephilimic version of Lilith and Lilith as Adam's first wife. Here are a few that are different than those previously presented.

Hypostasis of Archeon- *Then the female spiritual principle [Lilith#2] became a serpent.*

Antiquities of the Jews- Josephus wrote, *"But while all the living creatures had one language, at that time, <u>the serpent [Lilith#1/Samael], which then lived together with Adam and his wife, showed an envious disposition</u>, at his supposal of their living happily, and in obedience to the commands of God; and imagining, that when they disobeyed them, they would fall into calamities"*

Moses b.- *Both Samael, king of the demons, and Lilith were born as one in the form of the serpent [Lilith#2].*

Cave of Treasures- *And God took a rib from the loins on the right side of Adam, and He made Khawa from it: ---In this manner did Satan enter in the serpent and he saw Eve. Satan led her astray concerning that tree,* [If Eve was Eve, then Khawa must have been Lilith #2]

Generations of Adam [1-5]-*In the process of time, Satan beguiled the women, -- A son was born to my wife, Lilith. The countenance of my son Cain was not like ours. Then I took Eve as my wife.* [This Lilith is Lilith#2]

Something Strange about **that Lilith Girl**

Eve Seduced by a Serpent

This just makes me mad as many seem to struggle with the idea that a human would have sex with a snake. The Jewish Zohar doesn't help matters.

> ***Zohar 3:76****-After the Serpent [Samael/Lilith#2]* <u>*mounted Eve and injected filth into her, she gave birth to Cain.*</u> *From thence descended all the wicked generations in the world. And the abode of demons and spirits is from there and from his side. Therefore, all the spirits and demons have one half from man below, and the other half from the angels of the supernal realm.*

This verse clearly indicates that Samael/Lilith was a Nephilim. It also tells us that there was no question in the Jewish mind that Eve had sex with the Samael/Lilith pair.

The question is, *"Did Eve have sex with the [Lilith]serpent?"* The answer is yes and no. There is no way to have had sex with a snake and snakes did not have arms and legs during the Pleistocene. All of that mess is made up simply because of the Hebrew word for Serpent/Conjurer. This conjurer must have been very handsome and Eve became so infatuated with him, she would later be "PUNISHED" by having her love her husband. This next image that is supposed to be Eve getting seduced by a stupid snake is totally wrong.

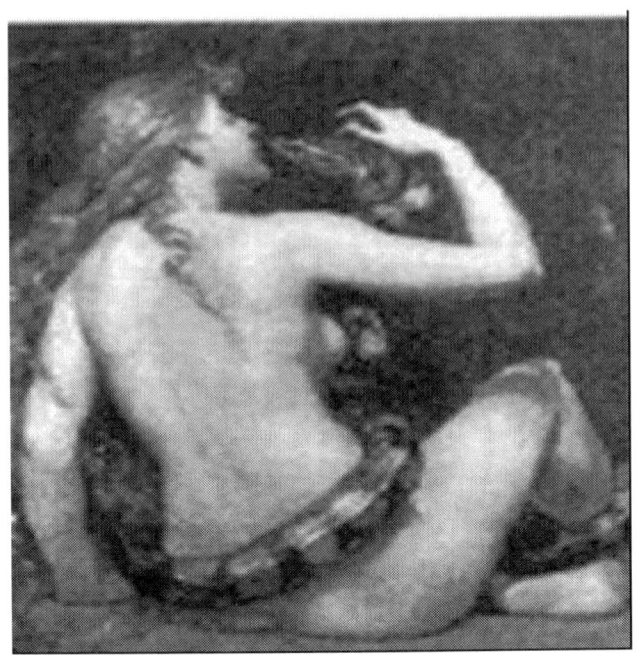

At times, through this history, it may seem that I am disturbing the "truth of the Bible". I Am Not. In, fact, I totally believe in its truth, but people should not put blinders on historical works because they feel that their minds could be changed. Truth will prevail and will only become clearer as more details are known. As shown in the picture above, early painters believed that Eve was more than just friendly towards a particular snake. At best, the historical answer to the question about serpent sex is, "possibly she did." --and the Bible does not discount that possibility.

Of course, she didn't have sex with a snake.

The creature depicted as a serpent might have been a substantially different creature. Ancient historical records and even the Bible give us indications that the creature called the serpent did, in all likelihood, have sex with Eve. Because she was enamored with the "serpent", she listened to him. In all likelihood, he was one of the "Nephilimic Beings". The book of Genesis indicated this Conjurer was *"more cunning than all the creatures"*. Adam and Eve learned from him/her. A more figurative way to say it is that they ate from the tree-of-knowledge. Let's use the ancient texts to help us decide the sex question. We also may gain insight concerning whether there was an actual "Tree-of-Knowledge" in the Garden of Eden.

Genesis 3:7-14- *And the eyes of them both were opened, and they knew that they were naked; and they sewed fig leaves together, and made themselves aprons.--And the woman said, the serpent "beguiled" me.*

To beguile someone is more than just deceiving them. It is almost like hypnotizing them. So whatever the serpent did it made Eve do whatever he wanted.

Eve could not control herself.

I know that doesn't necessarily mean having sex, but for some reason, she decided to cover her genitals after the incident. I know you're still thinking that this is stupid as a woman could not have sex with a reptile, but before we get into that concern, let's look at other examples of the same incident. They are much more descriptive. They may provide a better picture, or, at least, will provide additional information from which to make up our own minds.

Enoch 68:6-7- *The name of the third is Gadrael: he discovered every stroke of death to the children of men. He Seduced Eve.* [Gadrael is associated with Satan and with the combination being Samael and Lilith]

Apocalypses Moses 19:3-[*Eve swore and oath to the serpent]* "*by the Cherubim and the tree of life! I will give* *also to my husband to eat"-and when he receive the oath from me, he went and poured upon the fruit the poison of his wickedness, which is lust, the root and beginning of every sin, and he bent the branch on the Earth and I took of the fruit and I ate.* [The only reason for the "LUST" word here is a reference to inappropriate sex with a Lilith-serpent.]

Jasher 2:9- *And the serpent, which God had created with them in the Earth came to them to entice them to transgress the command of God, and the serpent enticed the woman to eat from the tree of knowledge, and she ate, and she took from it and gave it to her husband.* [Again no direct accusation of sexual encounter is found here, although entice is also a very strong word of control.]

Jubilees 3:21- *-- and she took thereof and eat. And when she had first covered her shame with fig-leaves, she gave thereof to Adam and he eats, and his eyes were opened, and he saw that he was naked. And he took fig-leaves and sewed them together, and made an apron for himself, and covered his shame.* [Why was Eve ashamed of her genitals, you might ask? We will also address Adam's shame.]

Jewish Tradition- *One of Satan's lieutenants named "Nahash" seduced Eve.* [This is a particularly interesting verse in that the word Nahash is almost identical with Nachash, the Hebrew word for serpent. Evidently the Lilith Serpent seduced Eve."]

Pelagasian Creation Story- *A serpent named Ophion coupled with the first woman.* [Ophion is one of Lilith's many names. This one is from the South Seas.]

Serpent Half-Breed

Most of the ancient Jewish texts indicate that Eve did have sex with this Lilith/Samael character and from their union came that very well-known murderer Cain. I know that the current Bible only indicates that Eve was seduced or beguiled by the serpent, but the texts below, put a more direct spin on that word seduced. Below are just a few of the texts connecting Cain with Lilith and Eve with the Serpent. The following text include some from Jewish Gnostic/Pharisee, Jewish Essene, Jewish Cabala.

Zohar 1:37*-When Samael [the serpent] mounted Eve, he injected his filth and she conceived and bare Cain.*

Eliezer 21*- The serpent came into her and she became pregnant with Cain.*

Philip 61:5*-First adultery came into being, afterward murder. And he [Cain] was begotton of adultery, for he was the child of the serpent. So he became a murderer, just like his father, and he killed his brother.*

Tertullian*- [Eve] Having been made pregnant by the seed of the devil she brought forth a son.*

Targum*-Adam knew about his wife Eve that she had conceived by Samael the wicked angel of God. He resembled the upper ones and not the lower ones.*

Patience 5:15-*[talking about Eve] Having been made pregnant by the seed of the devil—she brought forth a son [Cain].*

Origin of the World- *Now, Eve is the one who, without a husband, bore her first offspring. "It is my husband who bore me; and it is he who is my father and my lord. yet I have borne a man as lord."* [According to this ancient work, Adam wasn't Cain's father.]

Cave of Treasures- *In this manner did Satan enter in the serpent and he saw Eve. Satan led her astray concerning that tree, straightway she plucked the fruit and ate and Adam, also did eat thereof. When he had eaten he also became naked.* [It really doesn't say why Adam and Eve became naked.]

Hypostasis of the Archons-*They expelled Adam and his wife [Lilith#2] from the Garden. Afterward his wife bore Cain and then Abel. --Adam THEN knew his female counterpart, Eve and she bore Seth to Adam* [His female counterpart, Eve, was not his wife until after these verses.]

Genesis 4:1-2- *And Adam knew Eve his wife; and she conceived, and bare Cain, and said, I have gotten a man from the LORD And she again bare his brother Abel.* [Although we typically consider that if Adam "Knew" his wife, then Cain must have been his child, but is that necessarily so? In this verse, the word lord is not accompanied by the word God, it should not be assumed that this master was the Lord God. The two entities, "lord" and "lord God", seem to be separated on purpose in the first few chapters of Genesis so that the reader would see them as two separate beings.]

Genesis 5- Whenever Seth, Eve's third child, was born, the Bible specifically identifies that Seth looked like Adam, while no such identification was given to either Cain or Abel. One way for a child not to look like the husband of the mother is that he was not the father.

Generations of Adam 4:1-3 and 5:1-9*-A son was born to my wife, Lilith. --Then I took Eve as my wife. A son was born to Eve whom we named Abel. Abel had been born of the Elohiym.* [Lilith was Adam's 1st wife and Eve was his second by this document.]

Lilith and her brother Samael- had sex with Eve and convinced her to eat of the Tree of Knowledge, Whenever she did, she found out that having sex with anyone that comes around was not a good thing, especially when her lover was Lilith.

Adam and Eve Find a Fig Leaf

So Adam and Eve were finding themselves sexually and sometimes inappropriately with Nephilim. Those acts were the reasons that both Adam and Eve felt they should cover their genitals when God confronted them, not because they thought that that particular part of their body was ugly. Think about what the Biblical verse says:

Genesis 3:7 *The eyes of both of them were opened and they knew that they were naked. They sewed fig leaves together and made themselves **loin cloths**.*

The most reasonable place to cover if you were ashamed would be your head. They had witnessed every animal having sex with one another and knew that sex in itself was nothing to be ashamed of. They would not have covered their genitals because they thought that that part of the body was supposed to be covered.

The only reason that they would have covered that body part is that it was doing something it wasn't supposed to do and that must have been having sex with the Nephilim.

You might wonder; how the Nephilim could have looked like reptiles? So further examination is required.

The Serpent Wasn't a Snake

Many use the serpent beguiling Eve as one of those reasons to dispute the truth contained in the Bible. Others like to use the snake sex as something ugly. All of the following seem to sound strange.

This creature was never in the Garden

- If the Serpent were a snake, then his brain would be too small to even think on its own enough to seduce a human.
- If his brain were shrunk along with his legs, the brain reduction would have been more of a punishment than the leg erasing and would have been mentioned.
- A serpent or reptile of any kind would never be a human's confidant or lover.
- Snakes have no vocal capability, beyond producing a hissing sound. Even speech seems ridiculous.
- Snakes or extremely shortened appendage reptilian creatures have been around for over 60 million years according to the fossil record.
- The "serpent" depicted in the Garden of Eden wasn't the forerunner of the snake as many have been told.

A Conjurer not a Snake

As I mentioned before. the Hebrew word interpreted in this instance for "serpent" is the word Nachash. Half the time it meant snake-like while the other half of the time it was interpreted to mean Conjure or Conjurer. The first description is stupid and the second one makes sense. There were, almost assuredly, already snakes in the garden and they did NOT have appendages as depicted below. While Adam and Eve were in the Garden, "Eve's serpent" was not scary, and was not ugly as depicted below. That creature would never have been able to become Eve's confidant. This version of Lilith, the serpent-like human that tempted Adam and Eve, was beautiful and handsome by all accounts. [He/she probably had some reptilian characteristics, but by most evidence, generally speaking, he looked like a human.]

Snakes had been in existence well before the time of the garden. The "serpent/conjurer" was most assuredly one of the "non-creating" Nephilim that were worshiped as gods. For our purposes, we will call her Lilith. When he/or she lost the capability of procreating with other humans and turned ugly, Adam and Eve were kicked out of the Garden while the serpent/conjurer evidently was not kicked out. Let's look at the Garden of Eden Serpent" and see how he/she ties into the punishment of the Conjurer for handing out forbidden fruit.

Lilith the Seraphimic Nephilim

This section is certainly going to sound strange, but there is proof of sorts. Jewish history tells of many types of beings. One of them was the Seraphim, while sometimes they were referred to as angels, they were certainly very different than those typically described as angels. Some of the seraphim angels would have become Nephilim after the Heaven war and that group is said to have been Reptilian or be able to shapeshift to appear more reptilian. This is where the reptilian people called Ubaid People come in as Lilith and Samael probably were Seraphimic and punished by having them ALWAYS appear reptilian.

 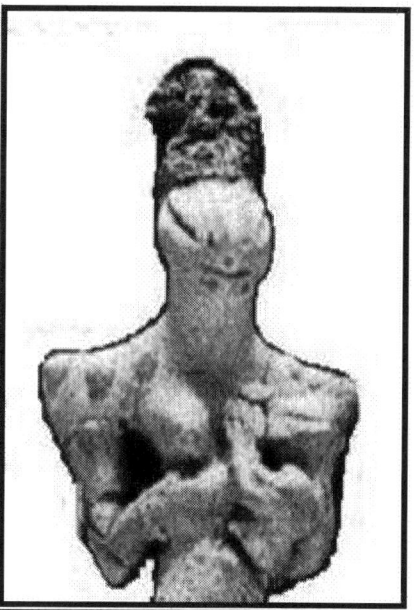

The Seraphim were, by all accounts, a special group of Nephilim that had obtained the capability of looking like reptiles or, by some mistake in their breeding actually looked reptile-like as shown above. They were sort of halfway between a reptile and a human. Believe it or not [don't you hate it when someone says that?] there are many, many examples of this strange type of human that lived with other "normal humans" a mere 5 thousand years ago. Reptile-like gods depicted by the ancients were usually depicted as being ugly. Like the one above, they all had broad shoulders and some type of insignias on their shoulders, usually with a pointed head and slanted "slit" eyes. While the "Eve confidant serpent-human" was probably not ugly, most of "his" descendants must have been considered less than beautiful. It appears that this "snake" was handsome until God got angry. According to the Bible, God gave him/her three punishments that affected human history.

- You will not be able to leave the earth [Dirt eating punishment]
- You will not be able to breed with other humans [Incompatibility punishment]
- You will become Ugly [Crushing Punishment]

Dust Eating Punishment

This over active Lilith-serpent was punished for his seduction. The first punishment was to make him/her eat dust. I'm sure you have been told that that means that the serpent's arms and legs were removed, but actually, it never says that. It simply says the conjurer would not go on his belly and eat dust.

Genesis 3:13-14*-And the LORD God said unto the serpent, Because thou hast done this, thou art cursed above all cattle, and above every beast of the field; <u>upon thy belly shalt thou go, and dust shalt thou eat</u> all the days of thy life.*

Most people use the model of a snake with arms losing them to become our present snake species as shown above, but that is a very simplified analogy to what larger act that occurred with the Seraphimic human. By many interpretative examples, one minute the serpent had appendages as shown in the first medieval painting and the next, she was without them as shown in the Greek depiction of their version of the Garden of Eden. Below is the Mayan Version with no arms.

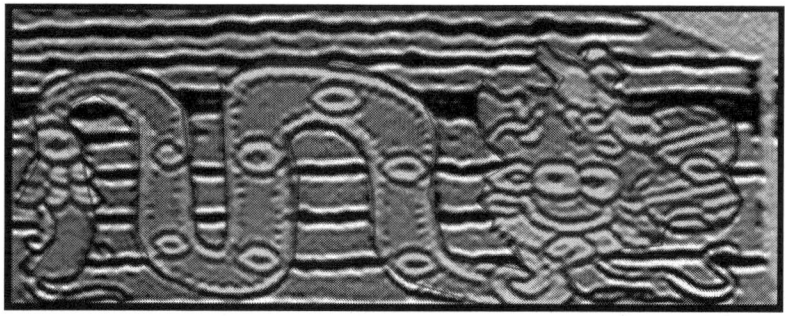

This depiction came from the Dresden Codex. He or she wasn't quite as pretty as depicted in medieval depictions, but the snake outfit is unmistakable.

Think about it. That interpretation makes no sense. This serpent guy didn't lose his appendages. I think a more realistic interpretation would be that this human would have to stay on earth, and he/she would have to stay in the form he was in {half human/ half reptile}. There have been way too many depictions of reptilian-like humans that have hands and feet to make me believe that all of the ancient people were wrong.

By the way the "can't leave the Earth" punishment was the basis for the 3rd emanation of Lilith which was the insatiable spirit wanderer looking for men to tempt. After death, Lilith could not leave the earth and had to stay here for an eternity just wandering.

Incompatibility Punishment

God didn't think that the crawling thing was enough so the serpent got a second punishment. The punishment was that the serpent couldn't have sex with humans anymore.

The Bible says *"I will put enmity between thy [the serpent's] seed and her [Adamic human's] seed.*

Some claim that the word seed here means children, but the fact of the matter is that there is little strife between snakes and children any more than children have strife with any other creature that could harm them. Why would the Bible single out this one animal strife and not mention the others? The reason is that it has nothing to do with snakes. Therefore, it must have meant that the "Nephilim/serpent" and presumably the other Nephilim could not produce offspring from a union with the new humans any longer. More than likely this genetic change occurred in the Nephilim only. We find in other works that other Nephilim certainly were able to have sex with humans and produce offspring and this did not limit the hybrid Eljo from breeding with Adamic humans either.

Crossbreeding became a common practice before the time of the huge flood we all have been told about, but the Seraphimic type Nephilim had to get trickier because of God's third punishment. As this medieval bronze carving shows, without her arms, Lilith, as the Serpent could not have sex and could not continue as a confidant of Adam and Eve. The depiction and similar ones are right about not being able to make babies, but the depiction is totally wrong about what Lilith's children looked like.

Crushing Punishment

God wasn't through with the serpent after the second punishment so a third one followed. God indicated that the woman would crush the serpent's head; the serpent would bruise her heel; and her desire would be only for her husband.

What is Meant by Crush?-For this, we need to take all three of the final statements:

- People will crush the head of the descendants of the Conjurer
- The Conjurer Descendants will bruise the heel of people
- Eve will now desire only her husband.

There is a reason that "desire for her husband" is mentioned with the other two. My belief is that the Nephilim still liked humans or, at least, felt a strong need to procreate with them. So this may be saying that the "new-breed" of "normal humans" would no longer like the Seraphimic type Nephilim physically----- they would be ugli-ated.

Seraphimic, Lilithian, Nephilim became Ugly

The Reptilian Nephilim probably became ugly at this time. That is why the Seraphimic gods are all depicted as being ugly. God didn't originally create them as being ugly, but the ugliness *"BRUISED THE SERPENT'S HEAD"*.

The Bible said about Eve, *"thy desire shall be to thy husband"*. If the "Seraphimic Nephilim" tried to have sex, the woman would not return affection any longer. It would be an emotional blow to the reptilian Nephilim. The literal translation of this Genesis verse doesn't work or snakes heads would be crushed in and women's heels would be bruised from crushing heads. Therefore, this interpretation may be what these verses are trying to say. By the way, this interpretation goes along with the Lilith story captured by the "Jewish Cabala", which indicated that Lilith had to get semen from men without their knowledge in order to create demons. Presumably, this was because men did not desire her. If she had been a Seraphimic Nephilim before the "Tree-of-Knowledge" fiasco, now she was an ugly Seraphimic Nephilim.

Codex Junius II- *The woman shall loathe thee under heaven. Her foot shall crush thy head and thou shall bruise her heel. There shall be strife between your seed forever.*

Genesis 3:15-*And I will put enmity between thee and the woman, ---This punishment shall bruise thy head, and thou shalt bruise common man's heel.- Thy [Eve's] desire shall be for thy husband only.*

You would think that after that horrible punishment Lilith would leave things alone, but she did not. It is believed she died well before Adam died and her daughter Naamah also died and they simply would not leave Adam alone. They came to Adam as demons and made his life miserable for a time.

Adam and Lilith

Eve wasn't the only one having sex with the Nephilim. Where ever she came from, many of the ancient texts talk about how Adam was with Lilith and one of Lilith's children when he wasn't with Eve. Here are a few of the texts which seemed to indicate that Lilith would not leave him alone even after death.

Lilith, Adam's Seducer

Zohar 1:54b-55a-*From the hour in which Cain killed Abel, Adam separated himself from his wife, [and] two female spirits [Lilith and Naamah] came and copulated with him. From the union he begot spirits and demons which roam in the world. This should not be difficult for you to understand, for when a man dreams, female spirits come and play with him and get hot from him and thereafter bear [those demons] which are called the Plagues of Mankind. And they turn into a likeness of men, but they have no hair on their head....*[I suppose it is saying to beware of baldheaded men].

Zohar 3:76b-*For 130 years, Adam kept separate from his wife and did not beget. After Cain killed Abel, Adam did not want to copulate with his wife. Rabbi Yose said: "From the hour in which death was decreed upon him and upon the whole world, he said 'Why should I beget children for terror?' and instantly separated from his wife." And two* *female spirits [Lilith#3 and Naamah] would come and copulate with him and bear children. and those whom they bore are the evil spirits of the world who are called the Plagues of Mankind. And they lead the sons of man astray, and dwell in the doorway of the house, and in the cisterns and in the latrines.*

Cabbalist Text-*From Adam's union with this demoness [Lilith], and with another like her named Naamah-Tubal Cain's sister [Adam's great- great- great grand-daughter], sprang innumerable demons that still plague mankind.*

Zohar 1:19c-*For 130 years Adam had intercourse with the female spirit [Lilith#2], until Naamah [She was a hybrid-partly from Adam and partly from Lilith] came. Because of her beauty, the sons of God [descendent of Adam] went astray-she bore from them and from her spread evil spirits and demons in the world. [These were in addition to the Nephilim who became demons when they died because of the ancient curse.]*

Biblical Text

Genesis 4:20:22-*And Zillah [Lilith-Lemech's wife], bore Tubal Cain and the sister of Tubal Cain was Naamah [According to the writing, this half-demoness had sex with Adam. She was his great- great- great granddaughter].*

Apocalypse Moses 5:1- *And Adam begat <u>thirty sons and thirty daughters</u> and Adam lived 930 [Jubilee] years [about 6500 normal years].*

Gnostic Text

Bacharach-*For evil Lilith [Lilith#2] came to Adam against his will and bore him many demons and spirits.*

Iranian Text

Mandaean tradition from Iran*-Ruha [Lilith#2] wished that she might have her own race and turned herself into a beautiful woman and said to Adam, "Come amuse yourself with me." Adam took her and became the father of children. The great men of old were the children of Adam and Ruha.*

About 10 thousand years ago the Earth shifted, the poles changed positions, and it rained for 40 days and 40 nights and then came massive earth-destroying, mile-high tidal waves as the poles repositioned. Just about everything and everyone was killed, but we are told about 120% of the Nephilim survived and a portion of those were the cursed descendants of Lilith. I would not be easy to be a descendant of Lilith. They were no longer the beautiful people.

Eve Has Cain

Before we go to the next section, let me tell you about a very, very strange verse in Genesis.

Genesis 4:4-7 *Eve conceived, and bare Cain, and said, I have gotten a man from the* LORD *[*NOT ADAM*].-- Cain brought an offering unto the* LORD ANd *Abel, he also brought - And the* LORD *had respect unto Abel--* <u>*But unto Cain - he had not respect.*</u>

Now that is certainly an odd verse!! From the other texts it is pretty clear that the Samael-Lilith combination was Cain's father so that was probably why God had no respect for him. I know some try to say God didn't like to have fruits and vegetables offered to him, but I think God liked them. He simply was worried about the DNA mismatch. While Cain produced Gentiles, Lilith descendants became something quite different.

Descendants of Lilith

Living With the Curse

As I mentioned, al of Lilith's descendants were cursed with Ugliness because of her part in the Tree-of-Knowledge debacle. When I say Lilith, I mean all of her clan or group or type. She may have been one of the Seraphim Angels before becoming a Nephilimic human. The reason this is a possibility, is we are told this group of angels were ugly and looked serpent-like, so after the fall of rebel angels. All the fallen were turned into Nephilim humans including the Seraphim ones. We can believe Lilith was one of these angels and all similar "Nephilim" were now stuck with reptilian features. There is indication this group survived up until about 5 thousand years ago, but they were certainly shunned by some. Like the others, when they died, they would have become demons. Below is a possible "after" picture of the once "beautiful" Seraphimic serpent/conjurer. While the picture is my interpretation, there are many examples that look similar of similar humans that lived during the ancient times. The word seraphim means "beings that warm" but we can imagine people simply running away.

According to Religio-historic documents, these ugly, six-winged, Nephilimic beings were high ranking, but ugly. Even though they were ugly, they were worshiped as gods and they generally helped other humans. I know it doesn't look like what you would think a person should look like but there is significant similarity in the descriptions and depictions of this human. At least know that they were ugly. These Seraphimic humans [ugly, reptilian-like or amphibian-like humans] have , actually, been worshiped many places. Here are a few of the more common depictions by those who had witnessed the seraphim or Ubaid people and wrote about them or made statues to them..

Don't Call a God Ugly

No one can convince me that someone would call a creature that they believed to be a god "ugly" unless they really were ugly. No one can convince me that there were not powerful and ugly people who were accepted into society at one time. There are just too many similar stories. Of course, we don't know that these scaly and ugly people were seraphim or the children of Lilith, but descriptions seem to point in that direction. They were called Oannes, Osiris, Seraphim, Ubaid, Nommos, and Gorgon. We find them covering themselves in Fish suits and Eagle suits, and displaying snake heads and 6-wings to assure us they were Seraphimic humans cursed to look reptilian.

Egyptian Seraphim Humans

Egyptians had their version of seraphim with multiple snakes around his human head and just like the Biblical description, these seraphim had 3 sets of wings. The picture to the left shows one of the humanoid creatures. He was ugly, [note the beetle body] but he was also powerful. His name was Osiris.

Middle Eastern Seraphim Humans

The Jews were certainly not the only people that wrote and told about an ugly god-like human that ruled over them during the ancient times. Here are a few of the more common examples.

Babylonians Seraphim Humans

OANNES and the other gods like him called the "Repulsive Ones", were honored by the Babylonians because they brought civilization. Sometimes they were depicted as humanlike beings inside fish outfits as shown, preceding right. Other times they were simply repulsive without a suit. Don't look at the aircraft on this depiction. That is another story.

Maybe the Nephilim had Help Living a Long Time

Speaking of another story, note the device in the center of the Babylonian stamping following [left]. This device was a common component of Babylonian and Sumerian depictions as shown again. The device must have been very important.

The Sumerians had the same depictions. Sometimes, somewhat unusual humans with wings and ugly beaks would come close to the object. Sometimes normal winged people would go over to it and point.

Some of the examples don't completely satisfy the details, but do have reasonable likeness. The Reptilian humans could very well have been the basis for these human depictions as well. I think you will see the punishment of Lilith in the Garden of Eden made her ancestors "distinctive".

American Seraphim humans

In the ancient Americas we find reptilian humans depicted everywhere showed slim, well proportioned, naked, wide shouldered with crimps or "bumps", well-proportioned bodies and reptilian-like heads. [See next left] Most were female, but some were male. Many had "slanted coffee bean" like eyes and erect hair. Some of the statues were even depicted suckling "ugly" babies.

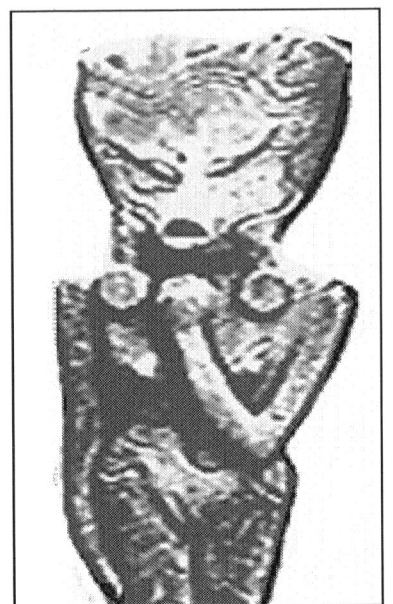 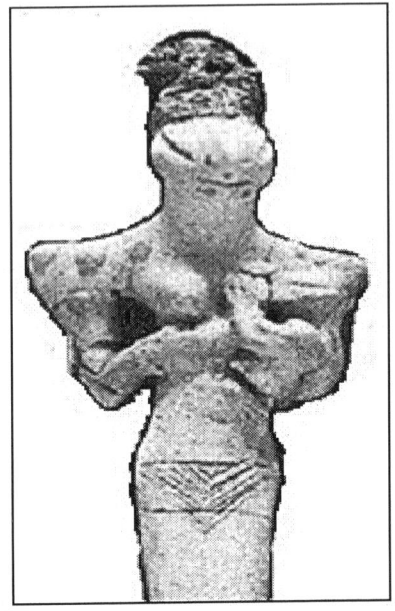

Mesopotamian Seraphim humans

Many of the writings discussing the strange Mesopotamian version of a Seraphimic human still remained intact. [See above right] Like those in the Americas, the ancient Mesopotamians made statuettes which also showed slim, well proportioned, naked, wide shouldered with 3 or 4 "bumps", well-proportioned bodies and reptilian heads. Again, most of those depicted were female, but some were male. Many had "slanted coffee bean" like eyes and a coil of erect hair. Like the one shown, some of the statues were depicted suckling babies. It should be noted that this type of person was well recognized and revered in ancient times.

Philistines-"Dagon and Atargis" were ugly, amphibious deities shown with tails of fish and human bodies. While there is a difference, these humans were also considered ugly.

Seraphim Humans in Western Africa

Dogon-NOMMOS gods were ugly and lived in the water. They were amphibious, but helped men. Like other Seraphim, Nommos were teachers. Their depiction is shown below left. They looked more like an ugly fish than a person.

Seraphim in Southern Africa

Nigeria-This Nigerian Snake God is certainly a Seraphimic creature as depicted in the middle and right above.

Seraphim Humans in India

Hindus-Vishnu, was a god-man who was, sometimes, half-man, and half-fish. In his first avatar, he was as the great fish Matsya as shown in this 18th century drawing [Next Left].

Greek Seraphim humans

Gorgon- With her snake hair and awesome power, Medusa and the other Gorgons were probably depictions of the ugly reptilian seraphim. [Preceding right]

Nersus- The snake god founder of Greece was most likely a Seraphimic human. Notice his non-human tail.

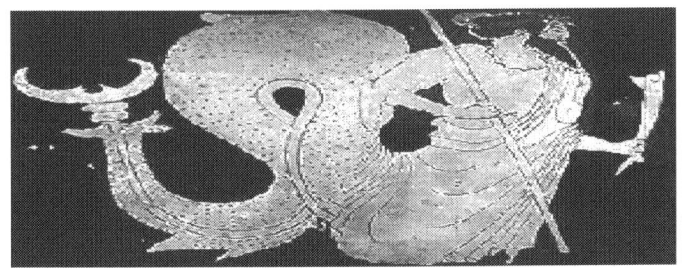

Japanese Seraphim human?

In Japan, they were called the Kappa. These amphibious "gods" lived underwater, had fins of some kind, and taught people agriculture, weaving, and poetry. Like the Nommo, they fit the characteristics of the seraphim, but these mischievous and ugly creatures also carried people underwater to their death. Next is a depiction of this ugly god. [I know he's riding a pickle, but that doesn't mean he didn't exist.]

Here is an overview of these powerful people shunned by many and feared by others.

Country	Greece	Greece	Egypt	Nigeria	Jewish
Name	Nersus	Gorgon	Osiris	Snake god	Seraphin
god or angel	X	X	X	X	X
Reptilian	X	X	X	X	X
Repulsive	X	X		X	X
Revered Teacher	X	X	X	X	X
Would kill	X	X	X	X	X
Had a Tail	X			X	X
Wings			Yes[6]		Yes [6]

Country	Japan	Babylon	India	Dogon	Philistine
Name	Kappa	Oannes	Vishnu	Nommos	Dagan
god or Angel	X	X	X	X	X
Reptilian				X	
Amphibian	X	X	X	X	X
Ugly/ Repulsive	X	X	X	X	X
Revered Teacher	X	X	X	X	X
Would kill	X			X	
Had a Tail			X	X	X
Wings		yes			Yes

Lilith's descendants were found everywhere. They even had families

Families of Lilith Descendants

The whole issue of Seraphic human procreation has been sidestepped in this work mostly to concentrate on less ugly humans. The survivors of the worldwide flood certainly procreated. This group of Lilith descendants may not have been pure Nephilimic, but they certainly had Nephilimic ancestors. These unusual humans had been seen by many and were similar to us except that they had large almond shaped eyes, very broad shoulders, large heads, and their almost reptilian like facial characteristics. The humanoid depicted in the dozens of sites are almost assuredly a real race of people in that identical descriptions and statues of these "people" can be found around the world. These humanoids may give us direct examples of procreation of those who were cursed by Lilith and Samael's actions in the Garden of Eden.

Pakistan & Iraq Reptilian People

The next 2 images are examples as depicted about 6 thousand years ago. The family on the left evidently lived in Mohen jo- Daro [Pakistan] while the mothers and babies depicted on two separate statues on the right came from a very ancient site in Iraq.

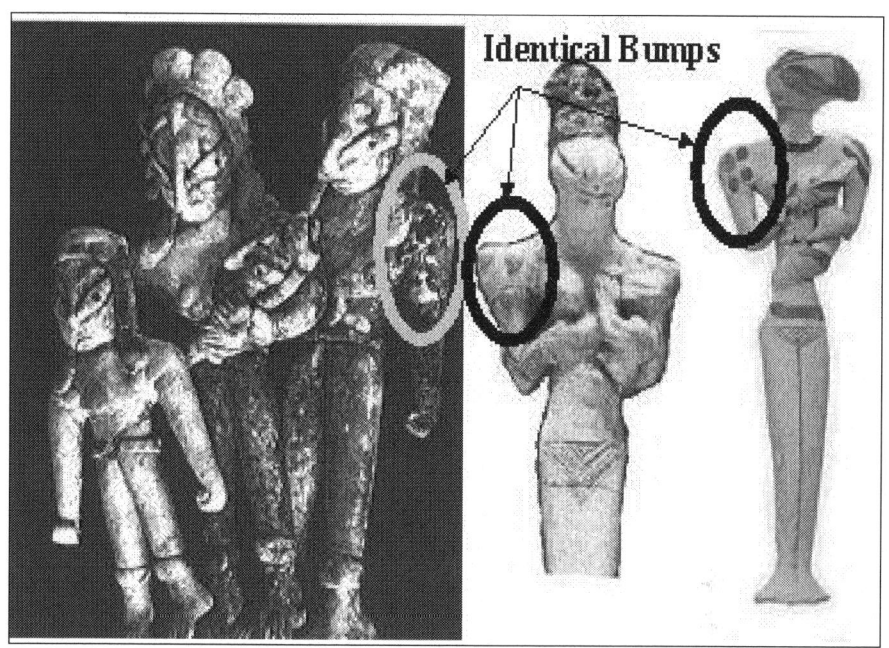

Note the large bumps on the shoulders of both groups. I have no idea what they represent, but there is no doubt that both examples depict the same species and little doubt that they are partially reptilian in appearance. By these and other similar depictions, we may believe that the ugly Lilith-ites might not have been able to breed with less ugly humans so they found a way to breed among themselves.

More Reptilian Humans

Mexico -The pictures below are, evidently, examples of these humanoid creatures. They are some of the ancient inhabitants of Mexico. While Middle Eastern Seraphimic humans have bumps on their arms, most of these have crimp marks. Many of the other characteristics to show that these are all depictions of the same humanoid. The one most noticeable is that they are ugly. Note that the second one has a child and he is ugly as well.

In Peru- As we look further at the Americas we find more. On the plains of Nazca, we find a human with the same "Bumps" on his arm and no significant nose. This characterization may indicate that the Reptilian humans inhabited that area as well. [Below left]

Saqqara Egypt- Let's look at one of the depictions from one of the tombs at Saqqara. No one can make me believe that this was a "Normal" human. The "look like a reptile" punishment had covered the globe. These people apparently were Lilith's descendants. They had made peace with their predicament and had integrated with the other humans, but there can be no mistake that they remained different. [preceding right]

Sumeria- Some of the artists tried to make these reptilian humans more appealing. The faces are sometimes smooth, but the characteristics are unmistakable. The long head, almost no nose, coffee bean eyes and bumps on the shoulders give them away as not quite human looking. The picture to the right is one of these depictions.

 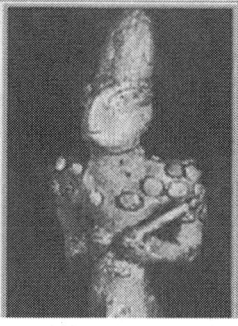 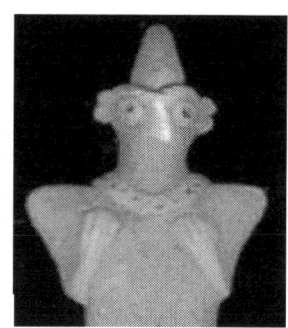

More Sumeria-The male below must have been highly decorated as he has more bumps on his arms that all the others. [Above middle] Still another Sumerian depiction of a "not quite human" image is shown to the right. While this image has a more normal nose, it is clearly a different type of humanoid. The extremely broad shoulders, pointed head, amplified eyes all appear to be depictions of this unusual human. I know he has a nose, but he certainly was an odd looking human.

Sumeria-The eyes of these "different" people may have been the element of most concern or fear or awe by the "normal" humans and the ancient Sumerians began building effigies with only the eyes of the person/god were evident as shown. Besides the pointed head version, the Big eyed, almost no head version of "unusual human type seems to have been a common cousin that also lived with "normal humans" .

Even More Sumeria-These eye sculptures were everywhere in ancient Sumeria and Babylonia. Below are a few of the strange eyed "gods".

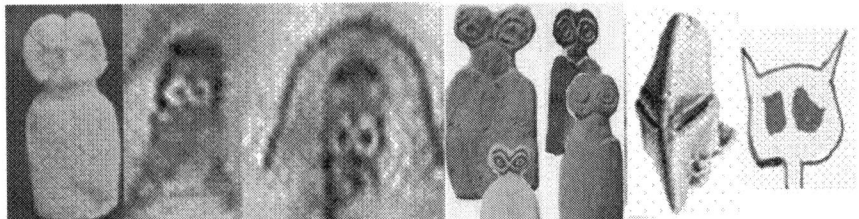

Iraq-Other sites in ancient Iraq yield more evidence that this unusual humanoid was lived among the homo-sapiens. This particular one doesn't have the characteristic bumps, but there can be little doubt of similarity. Don't let anyone tell you that the ancient artisans simply couldn't depict a human face. Many of the ancient depictions are of normal humans and are characterized as such. These were simply different looking individuals.

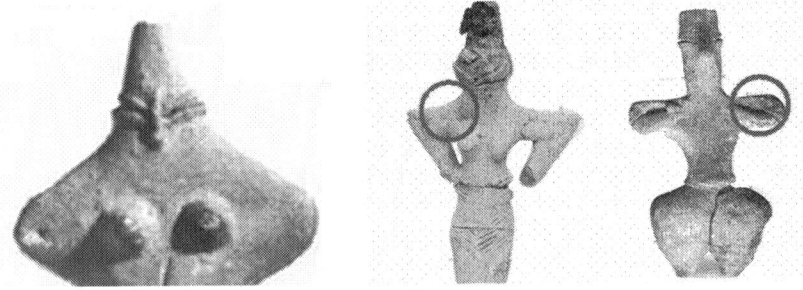

Pakistan and Greece-Still more images of these strange individuals have been uncovered. The one in the middle is still another from ancient Pakistan while the one on the right was found in Greece. The bumps are very noticeable on the Pakistani version.

Iran-In several ancient sites in Iran scientists have uncovered a large quantity of these remarkable humanoid figures. Some are shown next. Some have bumps on the arms, but all seemed to be similar in facial characteristics. Extremely pointed heads and almost a beaklike appearance must have made these individuals stick out from the normal humans of the day. The swastikas on the arms didn't mean the lizards headed individuals were Nazi as sculptures were completed some 6 to 8 thousand years ago.

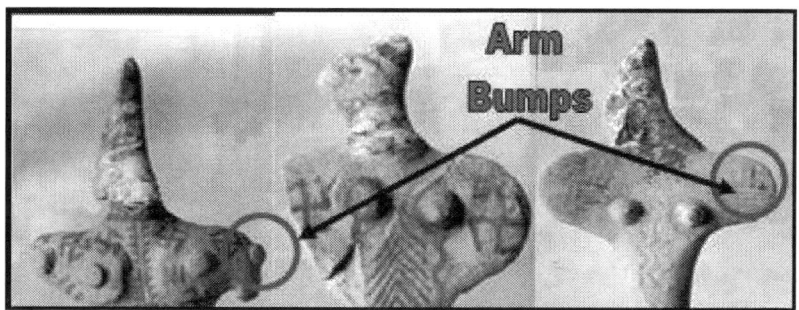

More Iran-It is obvious in the bowl depiction found in the ancient city of Uruk in Iran that the unusually long face was not that of a normal homo-Sapien either. These guys must have been everywhere.

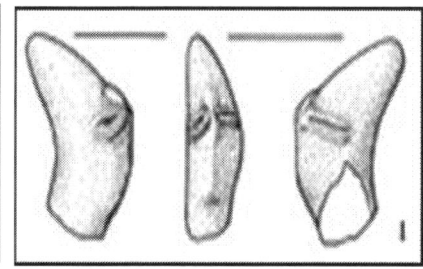

Turkey-As we go to the Amuq plains in southeast Turkey, the same type individual was depicted. The sketch above shows the face of this "not quite human" person.

Australia-Besides the entire Middle East, Europe, and the Americas, we find the same being may have been revered in the Australian Islands. Depicted as a god, humanoids with similar features inhabited that area of the world as well. [See next left]

In Australia we also find other similar beings. They seem to have reptilian features- Almost no nose and large eyes. No one knows what the spikes are on the head, but I bet you would recognize these gentlemen in a line-up.[Below right]

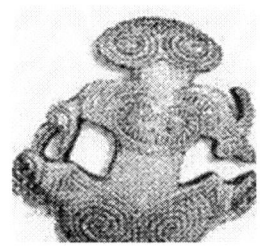 

Japan- was no exception. They had similar citizens. Dozens of these characteristic beings were depicted in that country during ancient times. Some have indicated that these are all Japanese because of the slanted eyes, but Japanese don't generally wear oversized goggles. In fact, Japanese aren't even reptilian as these appear to be.

Some have identified these as normal men wearing space suits or underwater gear, but the last of the group is definitely female and she seems to be wearing a skirt and a lot of jewelry. Hardly a space suit. The figure in the middle of the bottom row has an exposed belly button which also seems to be inappropriate for a special suit. These guys just were ugly I reckon.

In Nepal, we find a similar human depicted on an ancient Plate-big head and eyes, almost no nose. The image the reptilian human characteristics.

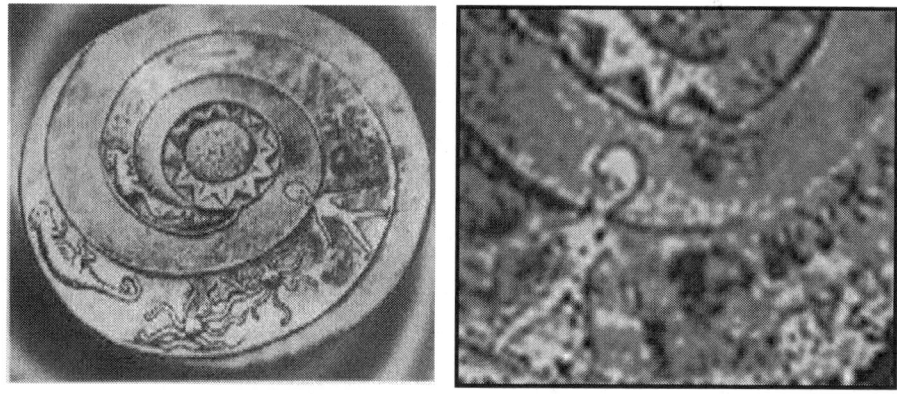

Possible Skulls

Brazil-We may even have one or two of the skulls. To the left is a skull found in the Serra do Machado area of the Amazon. Please note the fanged teeth, the flared areas under the eyes and the huge eye sockets. This massive skull did not come from a regular human. He would possibly have looked reptilian.

In Peru was found a slightly different skull, shown in the middle, but the large eye sockets show us that this is a different type of human before his skin came off. Neither of these skulls is of a pointed head being, but what about the last one. This one was also found in Peru and might have been an example of a reptilian human, punished for his ancestor's actions in the Garden of Eden.

Over time the Ugly descendants would have died off and people would begin to take even more latitude in what these people looked like. I call this next section "Serpent gods".

Serpent Gods

While at first you would think it to be stupid to believe that serpents were supernatural, but the evidence can be found around the world. The offspring of Lilith's group would probably have still known the secrets of the ages and lived extremely long times--- they just were ugly while living.

Why would a lowly creature like the snake be so revered, unless there was something special about reptilian-like beings in the early days. No matter what the reason was, everyone began to believe that snakes were gods. Here are some of the snake gods from around the world.

Far Eastern Serpent Gods

India- "Manasa" the goddess of snakes protects children.

Indian Serpent God.

This nine headed serpent controlled life itself. To the right of the nine headed serpent are more examples of Snake gods of India.

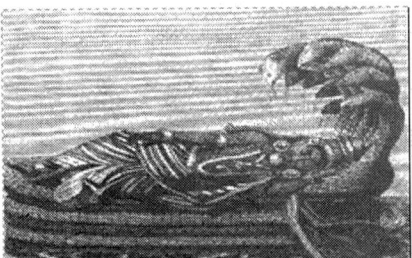

Hindu- The seven headed snake called Narayana represented the seven planes and elements.

Buddhist- The seven headed serpent called Naga sat under the tree-of- life to protect it. [Sounds like the seven headed serpent from Mayan history doesn't it. Even the name is the same]

Pakistan Serpent God

In ancient Mohen jo Daro [Pakistan] the serpent guarded a "tree-of-life as shown below left. The fish sign means Star or heavens. [It possibly means that the tree of life was taken up to heaven as indicated in some of the early writings]

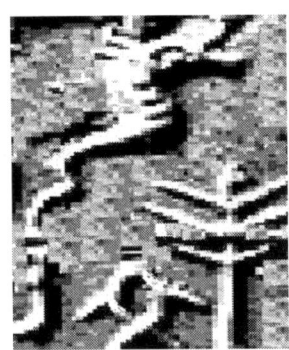

Araucanian [Chile] Serpent God- The Cherrie were the spirits of the shooting stars. They were depicted as man headed serpents on pottery.

Central American Serpent Gods

Aztecs & Toltecs- Quetzalcoatl was the serpent god.

Maya- The seven headed serpent called Naga guarded the life principle.

European Serpent Gods

Lithuania- Zaltys was the grass snake deity and symbol of fertility—Aspelenie took the form of a serpent and was the goddess of the Earth.

Greece- The Caduceus was a staff with two entwined snakes, which provided inviobility. Hydra was a seven headed serpent god as shown above right.

Basque- Herren-Surge was a devilish spirit in the shape of a seven headed snake. Maju is the divine spirit of the storm and takes the form of a snake.

Pacific Island Serpent Gods

Haiti- Damballah-Wedo- the most popular god takes the form of a snake.

Melanesia- Koevasi is the Melanesian snake goddess-Walutahanga was born to a mortal female, but was a female snake.

New Guinea- The sun god Yarhibol is portrayed as a giant Snake.

Middle Eastern Serpent Gods

Iran- In the Zoroastrian text, Bundahishu, says that *Angra Mainyu, the evil spirit and father of Daevas, had the appearance of a serpent with legs.*

African Serpent Gods

Mali- Nommo is half man and half snake. He represents the totality of the cosmos. [These Nommo were indicated in Hittite history as well and are very similar to the Dogon description.]

Zulu tribe-The creator was a lizard human [just like the Dogon tribe history].

Dinki Tribe, Africa- According to tradition the first woman, patron goddess of the garden was in the form of a snake [sounds like Lilith in the Garden of Eden to me].

The Egyptian God [Nephilim] Isis

Isis is sometimes connected with Lilith. She could transform to a serpent according to ancient texts. Here she is as a snake. Also, the Creator, Kneph, was shown in the form of a snake.

Most People were "Normal"

Before I end this book, here are a couple of "normal human" statues found at one of these same sites. Note the lack of bumps on the shoulder. They also don't have a lizard look or tiny slits for eyes. The hair on these statues has long since eaten away, but it's easy to see that the people of that time were depicted in sculptures as normal. Only the strange looking humanoids were depicted strangely. I can't comment on the breast holding . What I can comment on is that the real reptile-like people were still very skilled in many things and were again worshipped as gods. The characterizations of these gods over time were changed, but the essence remained the same, the gods were partially reptilian. Around the world, the worship of reptilian-like gods abounded.

When they died, just like all Nephilim humans, they could never leave the Earth. They were stuck here as demons, living a life in-between reality. From descriptions and depictions we can understand quite a bit about Lilith as she went from life to something different than life.

Lilith#3 As A Demoness

Lilith#3 in the Cabbala

The Jewish Cabbala Texts provide a substantial amount of information concerning Lilith. If we go back a little; in those stories, Cro-Magnon man "Adam" wanted to be in control, but the Nephilim, Lilith, wanted to be in control also. Therefore, the Nephilim went away and the Adamic men stayed by themselves. The Nephilim were still in the same boat they had been in . When they died, they became demons. To counter that, every effort to breed with Cro-Magnon was a pushed hard. While that would not work, they were successful in breeding with the Cain-ites and Gentile, but after death, they still became demons. Oh! Well! Lilith demons decided to wreak havoc on the populations of the world. Lilith became so scary, men would not go to sleep without reciting incantations to keep Lilith and her demons away.

Lilith the Demon Maker

One of the aspects of the ancient stories is that Lilith tried to have children, but Lilith's children were all killed by the angels of God. She would continuously get sperm from unsuspecting men to have more and more children. The offspring that survived, according to the stories, turned into demons rather than normal children. By the way; the way she got sperm was from men having nocturnal emissions, so early Jewish men were afraid to go to sleep, fearing that they could become the fathers of demons. It was even worse than that because Lilith would, many times kill the male donor after getting her prize.

Lilith & the Sumerians

In the "Gilgamesh Epic", Lilith lived in a tree [similar to the tree-of-life] in the god's garden [similar to the Garden of Eden]. Her depiction is shown next.

The Epic of Gilgamesh-And <u>Lillake [Lilith] was the demoness dwelling</u> on the trunk of the willow tree-tended by

the goddess Inanna. [We will see this same demoness in the tree theme throughout most of the Jewish stories.]

Sumeria, Akkadia, & Babylon

Whether she was called Lilla, Ilitu, or Ishtar, the Sumerian descriptions have striking similarities to other Lilith images.

- **Sumerian-** Lilla- the night demoness
- **Akkadian**-Ilitu- the night demoness
- **Babylon**-Ishtar—she was an evil temptress, heartless. She would generally destroy her lovers.

Just like the Jewish version, Lilith was associated with Owls shown at her feet.

Jewish Demon Making Lilith

Ancient Jewish texts went further. They developed a whole demon culture around the belief that Lilith was an evil and powerful being.

Bacharach, 19 - *And behold, the harsh husk, that is Lilith, is always in the sheet of the bed of a man and a woman who copulate, in order to take the sparks of the drops of seed which go waste, because it cannot be without this, and she creates from them demons, spirits and Lilin. And there is an incantation to drive away Lilith from the bed and to bring forth holy souls, which is mentioned in the holy Zohar.*

Bacharach, 102-103- *The Alien Woman is Lilith, and she is the sweetness of sin and the evil tongue. And from the lips of the Alien Woman, honey flows. And although the Impure Female has no hands and feet for copulation, for the feet of the serpent were cut off, nevertheless the Female in her adornments looks as if she had hands and feet. And it is the mystery of her adornments that she can seduce men.... And* *she leaves the husband of her youth [Samael] and descends and fornicates with men who sleep below in the impurity of spontaneous emission, and from them are born demons and spirits and Lilin, and they are called the Sons of Man.*

I know all of the Lilith stories are confusing, but ancient historians thought that she was very important to the ancients and she was closely tied to Adam. I have brought out differing versions of this Lilith character so that you could make your own determination. While we are discussing Lilith, we must look at Cain as well, because Lilith could have been his mother. We'll get back to that in a little.

Lilith the Evil Spirit

The Cabbalistic Lilith description was expanded to include a hostile Nephilimic being bent on producing hybrid beings whether humans wanted her to or not..

The Early Jews feared Lilith greatly and continuously warned against this female who became a night stalker many thousands of years after the time of Adam.. They made up methods to keep her away and told stories of people who were victorious over Lilith. As you read these sections it may seem somewhat comical, but in all the fear and symbolistic writing, there are details that we can glean. Here are some of the details provided in the Zohar texts of the ancient Jewish Cabbala. Of course, these mystic renditions should be taken with a grain of salt, but they should not be ignored, because there is some truth in them.

Lilith, the Temptress of all Men

Zohar 1:148b*-Two evil spirits joined :the spirit of the male [the Samael character] is subtle; the spirit of the female [Lilith] is diffused in many ways and paths but joined to the spirit of the male. She bedecks herself with all kinds of jewelry like an abhorrent prostitute posing on the corner to seduce men.*

The fool who approaches her Seeing him stray from the path of truth, she strips herself of all her finery that she dangled before that fool, her adornments for seducing men: her hair all arranged, red as a rose, her face white and red, her mouth poised, a delicate opening.

The tongue pointed like a sword, her words smooth like oil, her lips beautiful, red as a rose, sweet with all the sweetness of the world. She is dressed in purple. He fornicates with her, deviates after her. She leaves him sleeping in bed.

She ascends [Lilith gains audience in heaven], denounces him, obtains permission, and descends. That fool wakes up and plans to play with her as before. But she removes her decorations and turns into a powerful warrior confronting him.

Arrayed in armor of flashing fire, his awesome terror vibrates the victim's body and soul. He is full of fearsome eyes; in his hand, a sharp-edged sword drips bitter drops. She kills that fool and flings him into hell. [I knew she was mean]

Jacob descended to her and was saved from her. [This is talking about the Jacob's ladder story]Her mate, Samael, was offended and swooped down to wage war but could not overcome him [This is also indicated in Genesis 32:25]

Zohar 1:54b-55a-*From the hour in which Cain killed Abel, Adam separated himself from his wife [Eve], and two female spirits [Lilith and Naamah] came and copulated with him.*

From the union he begot spirits and demons which roam in the world. This should not be difficult for you to understand, for when a man dreams, female spirits [Lilith and Naamah] come and play with him and get hot from him and thereafter bear those demons which are called the Plagues of Mankind.

And they turn into a likeness of men, but they have no hair on their head....[I suppose it is saying to beware of baldheaded men].

Lilith and Naamah Together

Zohar 3:76-*Thereafter Adam begot on those spirits [Mating with Lilith and Naamah] daughters who are the beauty of those above and those below.*

And all went astray after them.[the offspring of Lilith and Naamah] *and there was one male who came into the world from the spirit of Cain's side, and they called him Tubal-Cain* [Son of Zillah and Lamech {great, great grandson of Adam} according to the Bible].

And a female came forth with him, and the creatures went astray after her, and her name was Naamah. [Daughter of Zillah and Lamech according to the Bible] *From her issued other spirits and demons. and they hover in the air and tell things to those others found below.*

And this Naamah became aroused and adhered to her evil side. And to this day, she exists, and her abode is among the waves of the great sea. And she comes forth, and makes sport with the sons of man, and becomes hot from them in the dream, in that desire which a man has, and she clings to him, and she takes the desire and from it she conceives and brings forth other kinds into the world.

And those children whom she bears from the sons of man come to the women, and they conceive from them and bear spirits. And all of them go to Lilith the Ancient [Lilith], and she rears them.... And she goes out into the world and seeks her children. And she sees the sons of man and clings to them, in order to kill them, and to become absorbed into the souls of the children of the sons of man, and she goes off with that child.

But three holy spirits arrive there and fly before her and take that child from her and place him before the Holy One, Blessed be He, and there he studies before Him. [Many of the children are saved from this terrible existence by angels]

Zohar 3: *77-At times, it happens that Naamah goes forth into the world to become hot from the sons of man, and a man finds himself in a connection of lust with her, and he awakens from his sleep and takes hold of his wife and lies with her. And this desire comes from that lust which he had in his dream.*

Then the child that she begets comes from the side of Naamah, for the man was driven by his lust for her. And when Lilith comes and sees that child, she knows what happened, and she ties herself to him and brings him up like all those other sons of Naamah.

And she is with him many times, but does not kill him. This is the man who becomes blemished on every New Moon, for she never gives him up. [The whole lunar cycle is constantly provided in ancient texts just like the newer werewolf and vampire stories.]

For month after month, when the moon becomes renewed in the world Lilith comes forth and visits all those whom she brings up, and makes sport with them, and therefore that person is blemished at that time.

Zohar 2:267b-*And that spirit which is called Asirta [Lilith] becomes stirred up...and goes to the female who is beneath all females. And she is Lilith the mother of demons.*

And a man may become stirred up by that evil spirit called Asirta, which attaches herself to that man and ties herself to him permanently. And on every New Moon that spirit of evil appearance becomes stirred up by Lilith, and at time that man suffers harm from the spirit, and falls to the ground and cannot get up, or even dies [More meanness]

Zohar 3:76b-*And two female spirits [Lilith and Naamah] would come and copulate with him [Adam] and bear children. and those whom they bore are the evil spirits of the world who are called the Plagues of Mankind.*

And they [Lilith and the spirit of Naamah] lead the sons of man astray, and dwell in the doorway of the house, and in the cisterns and in the latrines.

Lilith Remedy

Not to worry, if Lilith of Naamah has come to a person, there was a cure. The cure could even be done before Lilith got to your family.

Zohar 3:19a-The remedy against Lilith is this: In that hour in which a man copulates with his wife, he should concentrate in his head on the holiness of his Master and say this: "O you who are wrapped in velvet, You have appeared! Release! Neither come nor go! Neither you nor yours! Go back! The sea is raging, Its waves call you, I hold on to the Holy One, Wrap myself in the King's holiness."

Then let him cover his head and his wife for one hour, and do thus each time for three days of the receiving. For a grafting which is not received within three days will not be received at all. But in the book which Ashmodai gave to King Solomon, it says for thirty days, and it says that after he finished the act he should sprinkle clear water around the couch.

We don't have Ashmodai's book, but it must also have been filled with this same level of demonology mixed with only a small amount of history. What we can tell is that this whole Lilith trying to control all men was a very common belief during the time of King Solomon.

Cabbala Note

OK! There is not a substantial amount of information that can be gotten from the "Zohar" due to its integrated mysticism; but the intermingled references throughout the ancient times concerning Lilith help us understand possibilities that tie various histories together in a reasonable manner. The early Europeans heard the ancient stories about Lilith and began to make their own versions of the stories.

Demonic Lilith Characters

The stories spread around the world. Some of the more common Lilith entities are described below. The similarity to the original stories from the Cabbala are unmistakable. Trying to find the truth in this sea of reinvention might be difficult, but some level of truth must be in there somewhere.

African Ngombe Tribe Description

A magnificent Garden was made for man [The Garden of Eden was made.] *A female saw a hairy man in the forest* [Nephilim {Lilith} inbreed with primitive Homo-Habilis.]

She married him and removed his hair. [The hybrid man, Homo-Erectus, was created.] *The evil Ebenga, a serpent god, tempted/seduced the woman* [Lilith and Ebenga {Samael in other texts} join to become a serpent.]

Afterwards, her child brought witchcraft and misery into the world [The offspring of Lilith become demons, promote witchcraft and inflict misery.]

Hungary-Szepasszony- Female demon who seduces young men. [Below left]

Etruscan- Tuchulcha- night demoness of the underworld, a winged woman with snake hair. [Sounds like the predecessor to the Gorgons and Medusa. See preceding right]

Medieval European-Succubus- female evil spirit would visit men in their sleep and have sex. The men would, many times, not wake up from the ordeal. The succubus [female] and incubus [male counterpart] were similar in every way except for being male and female. [This is identical to the Jewish perception of what Lilith became after her eventual death.]

Other Depictions

We find that a vengeful, generally beautiful, female spirit has been seducing men and killing children around the world. At least that is the story being told. Below are a few of the many Spirit Lilith depiction and their similarities.

Where	Name	Vengeful Female	Spirit form	Beautiful	after children	seduce or kill men
Arabic	Algul	x	x	x		
Aztecs	Civatateo	x		ugly	x	
Balkins	Bibi	x		x	x	
Europe	Succubus	x	x	x		x
Greece	Lamia	x		x	x	x
Greece	Mormo	x		x	x	
Iceland	Mara	x		x	x	x
India	Churel	x	x			
India	Rakshasa	x		x		x
Ireland	Dearg-due	x		x		x
Japan	Hannya	x	x	x	x	x
Java	SundalBolong	x	x	x		x
Malaysia	Penanggalan	x	x		x	
Malaysia	langsuir	x	x		x	x
Moldavia	Zmeu	x	x	x		x
Philippines	Aswang	x		x	x	
Philippines	Mandurugo	x	x	x		x
Russia	Vourdalak	x	x	x	x	
Russia	Upyr	x			x	
Sweden	Mullo	x		x		x
Togo	Adze	x	x		x	

I know this whole Lilith thing is confusing, but trying to put together historical puzzles can be like that. Sometimes Lilith was just evil, sometimes she was a Nephilim, and most of the time she was associated with serpents and gods or demons. The ancient people would not have written so much about her is there wasn't some truth in it. They also would not have had so much fear unless there was some catalyst at some point in time. Some portion of the Lilith saga must be true. It is up to you to try to determine what parts you believe. One area that is hidden often in our normal history textbooks is the insurgence of descriptions, and statues to honor or describe reptilian like humans that lived with others.

Whatever you want to call her, Lilith was an important person and concept in ancient times. She had been associate with all of the following:

- Genetic breeder of Humans
- Wife of Adam
- Father of Cain
- Serpent Temptress
- Punished Seraphimic Human
- Matriarch or the Reptilian Ubaid humans
- Mother of the Gentiles
- Mother of Demons
- Deadly Demoness of the night

With that, let's try to make some conclusions about this mystery woman.

Conclusion

The stories provided can be segregated into several parts and, hopefully, you have gained a better appreciation for the ancient texts in this overview. I have listed them below with a short synopsis.

People have been on the earth since the Mesozoic Era. [How they got hear wasn't covered, but it is my belief that the Creator God put them on the earth.]

Over that time, they gained a huge amount of knowledge concerning living longer and genetic manipulation. [This only makes sense as we have gained a considerable amount of knowledge in those areas in the very short "modern times"]

One of the genetic experiments was the changing of apes into men.

After many changes, these ancient humans began using their own DNA as a change catalyst. They may have even had sex with the experiments.

The result was a somewhat better humanoid. [I presented this as the Homo-Habilis ape-man]

Even this new man was not helpful in doing work for the ancient humans so God created a new human. [I presented this as the Homo-Erectus-first true human not associated with the ancient humans]

The ancient humans [Nephilim] bred with these humans and produced many different strains. [We called the breeder Lilith. One of these hybrid humans was called the Neanderthal man. He was a great worker, but not creative in any way. He also lacked appreciation of the Nephilim for "creating him".]

God was not impressed with the work that the Nephilim were doing and he created still another human [ADAM] with special qualities including an internal spirit that could travel to heaven.]

The Nephilim were at it again and one named Lilith bred with this new ADAMIC man.

God put a stop to the Lilith cohabitation with the purebred Adamics after the Garden of Eden fruit incident, but the hybrids could mate with the Adamics and they did-many times.

Most of the people of that time were from the union of Lilith or others like her and the small group of Adamic humans. [The Adamics were considered the Chosen ones. Noah and his family were the only chosen ones to survive the flood]

After the flood, some portion of the Nephilim survivors had been part of the sex with Adamics crime and had been changed to look like half human-half reptile. [We know that this group lived among the "normal humans" because of the great number of statuettes showing they lived, worked, had babies, and were evidently at peace with the "normal" humans for many years.]

By this time, Lilith and her offspring named Naamah had died, but their spirit was left on the earth to tempt men

and do other generally evil things. [This was a widespread belief of the Jewish community and it spread to many others. The truth of this cannot be determined as it gets into some weird things.]

Lilith, or several Liliths, seemed to have been mother of several forms of humans. She genetically manipulated human of ape-man beings. She bred directly with sub- humans and the descendants of Cain to produce the Gentile humans. She finally became a half reptile half human herself because of her inappropriate actions.

The hardest part of this story to believe is that humans actually were on the earth with the dinosaurs and could live for thousands of years. The strong evidence should make it more palatable, but you will have to accept the evidence and accept the historical portions of the ancient texts before you can make the step towards understanding Lilith.

The End

About the Author

Steve Preston is a long lime author of scientific, esoteric facts. His books focus on the painful truths rather than whitewashed details that make us comfortable. If you are interested in the truth instead of comfort, please review other works by Mr. Preston as shown below. The images are some from Egypt taking the older version of taxi. To the right the writer is shown in the Jewish Negev desert of Israel where the Dead Sea Scrolls were found.

 To the left below are a couple of pictures as we searched the New Zealand caves possibly visited by the ancient Maori and the last image is of the author investigating the statues on the Acropolis in Athens Greece.

History of Mankind Series
20th Century To The End Of Time
The Second Creation of Man
The Creation of Adam and Eve
A New View of Modern History
Close Look at Ancient History
The Antediluvian War Years
The First Creation of Man
Man After The Flood

Modern American Topics
History of Powerful Women
Promote the General Welfare
Modern Misconceptions
Our Very Odd Presidents
American School Disaster
The Bad Side of Lincoln
Can We Save America?
Great American Quiz
Humans on Display
Consensus Science
Monsters are Alive
US History Errors

Prehistoric America
Who Discovered the Americas?
Mysterious PreIncan Journey
Phoenicia and the Lost Jews
Romans found America

Prehistoric Technology
Amazing Technology
Mysterious Pyramids
Incredible Titans
Anakim Gods

Prehistoric History
Creation and Death of Dinosaurs
Kingdoms Before the Flood
When Giants Ruled the Earth
Not from Space

Reality Science Anomaly
Our 12-Dimensional Universe
Mystery of Photons and Light
Meaning of Life and Light
Incredible Nikola Tesla
Is Time Travel Possible?
Biophotonics and Healing
Vibrational Matter
Slip Through a Wall
Anthropic Reality

Historical Fiction
Conrad and the Flood
Secrets of Washington
Shama and the Tower
Naille and the Exodus
Religious Anomalies

Biblical History
Does Science Confirm the Bible?
History Confirmed By The Bible

Abraham to Moses
Adam to Abraham
Adam's First Wife
Moses to Jesus

Moses Studies
Moses Story Part 1
Moses Story Part 2
Expanded Genesis
Exploring Exodus
Exploring Genesis

Christian Studies
Differences in the King James Bible
Why the King James Bible Failed
Understand the New Testament
Old Testament Used By Jesus
New Testament Mysteries
Allah' God of the Moon
Errors in Understanding
Old Testament Mysteries
New look at the Bible
Incarnations of God

Biologic Anomaly
Tracing Cro-Magnon to Jesus
God Didn't Make The Ape
DNA of Our Ancestors
Homo Erectus as a Man
DNA Anomalies
Races of Men
Lizard People

Wars
America's Civil War Lie
Behind the Tower of Babel
World War with Heaven
Four Armageddons
World War Before

World War Zero
Six Deaths of Man
Driven Underground

Egyptian Studies
Truth About Hyksos Pharaohs
Scythians Conquered Ireland
Mysteries of the Exodus
Egyptian Foreigners
Moses Saved Egypt
Secrets of Thoth

Metaphysic Science Anomalies
Releasing Your Consciousness
Understand your Heart
Vampires among Us
Awaken the Departed
Self, Soul, Spirit
Life Resonance
Self-Virtualization
Of Heaven and Hell
True Happiness

Flight & Space Travel
Ancient History of Flying
Anomalies in Flight
Living on Venus
Space Anomalies
Where UFOs Go
Martians

Angels and Demons
Sex Crazed Angels
The Antichrist
The Devil

Made in the USA
Middletown, DE
03 February 2019